CONTEMPORARY PERSPECTIVES ON CATHOLIC EDUCATION

CONTEMPORARY PERSPECTIVES ON CATHOLIC EDUCATION

JOHN LYDON (ed.)

GRACEWING

First published in England in 2018
by
Gracewing
2 Southern Avenue
Leominster
Herefordshire HR6 0QF
United Kingdom
www.gracewing.co.uk

ISBN 978 085244 933 2

Typeset by Gracewing

Cover design by Bernardita Peña Hurtado

CONTENTS

INTRODUCTION

> At the root of Catholic education is our Christian spiritual heritage, which is part of a constant dialogue with the cultural heritage and the conquests of science; Catholic schools and universities are educational communities where learning thrives on the integration between research, thinking and life experience.[1]

THIS CITATION FROM Educating Today and Tomorrow, a landmark document published by the Congregation for Catholic Education prior to the eponymous World Congress 2015, encapsulates the nature and purpose of this book which, in essence, constitutes a dialogue between theology and education. The notion that the perennial, in the form of the rich heritage of the Catholic education tradition, must remain in constant dialogue with the transitional educational landscape permeates this publication which is rooted in a distinctive understanding of the human person and is anchored in three core principles: the dignity of the individual, the call to human flourishing and the promise of a divine destiny.

Contemporary Catholic Education was first published in 2002[2] focusing on Catholic education in the United Kingdom. The book addressed the context of Catholic education, its reality in the contemporary Catholic school and concomitant challenges viewed from the perspectives of the time. This book can be regarded as a sequel, extending beyond the UK to encompass perspectives from the Republic of Ireland, Australia and the USA. This book focuses on dialogue with the contemporary situations. Catholic schools and universities educate people, first and foremost, through the living context, that is to say, the climate that both students and teachers establish in the environment where teaching and learning activities take place.

The educational landscape since 2002 has experienced significant developments, first in relation to secularisation which James Arthur has claimed 'proceeds [in Catholic schools] at a dramatic pace with policy and practice consequently more distant than ever from the educational principles of Church teaching'.[3] Second, concurrent with an enveloping secularism, there has been a continuing and expansionist marketising of education marked by an enhanced focus on measurable outcomes and performativity. Third education structures are changing dramatically, for example in England where the role of Local Authorities as intervening institutions is being eroded by a more centralist model exemplified by the introduced of multi-academy trusts. In these contexts the value of the witness of a Catholic teacher is accentuated and, in the words of Pope Francis, 'teaching ultimately has to be reflected in the teacher's way of life, which awakens the assent of the heart by its nearness, love and witness'.[4] The importance of witness permeates this publication which is structured around three themes: context, Religious Education and Leadership and Governance.

In the first section Martin Browne in *Catholic Secondary Education in the Irish Context* begins by quoting Pope Francis who suggested that:

> today there is no great need for masters, but for courageous witnesses, who are convinced and convincing ... the most effective and authentic witness is one that does not contradict, by behaviour and lifestyle, what is preached with the word and taught to others! Teach prayer by praying, announce the faith by believing; offer witness by living![5]

Browne goes on to navigate the changing educational landscape in the Republic of Ireland, analogous to that in the UK before going on to explore teaching as a ministry in this changing context. Fr Ron Nuzzi, in a chapter entitled evocatively *A Balkanised Educational Landscape*, states in his introduction that 'free market forces, legislative changes, and an overall climate of increased accountability among educators, parents, and political leaders have initiated some disruptive innovation into the once stable system'. This statement, reflecting accurately the current locus of the English education system, is encapsulated in the word 'choice' which is cited 35 times by Fr Nuzzi and has enormous ramifications for Catholic education in the USA going forward. Christopher Richardson in *Researching Catholic Education* explores an alternative approach to researching Catholic education. It draws on the theoretical perspective and experience of those engaged in empirical theological research, which involves a synthesis of theology and the empirical methods of social science. Citing an impressive range of critical scholarship Richardson concludes by suggesting that such a synthesis involves a dialogue between this critical interpretation and the tradition of the Church leading eventually to renewed practice and experience.

The second part consists of a range of chapters on Religious Education with perspectives from England and Ireland. The Catholic Church has stated that Religious Education should be at the heart of the curriculum and should indeed be architectonic, reflecting the Congregation for Catholic Education's insistence that a school would not deserve the title Catholic if 'no matter how good its reputation for teaching in other areas there were just grounds for a reproach of negligence or deviation in religious education properly so-called'.[6] In a chapter entitled *Religious Education Reform in the Catholic Schools of England and Wales* Anthony Towey and Philip Robinson address issues around the introduction of a new Religious Education curriculum at Key Stages 4 (ages 14–16) and 5 (16–19 year olds) in England. Reform takes centre stage with the authors, who have represented the Catholic hierarchy in negotiations around the reform, articulating its rationale and purpose, navigating political, education and theological perspectives. Since Catholic students compose 25% of all pupils taking GCSE and 20% of all Advanced Level students, it is entirely appropriate that the Catholic Church, represented by the CREDO group, the provenance of which is discussed in the text, has played a key role in the drafting of the specifications. In a compelling account Towey and Robinson navigate the terrain

around the process of developing the specifications, encompassing immediate, medium term and long term issues. Reference to
the 'unprecedented levels of co-operation between policy makers,
advisers, practitioners and academics through the CREDO group'
is a particularly important claim in this very readable account of
a significant and potentially far-reaching curriculum innovation.

Amalee Meehan in *The Sickness of Long Thinking: Religious
Education and the New Junior Cycle* begins by addressing the
ongoing spiritual hunger in a Western culture which appears to
have lost its identity and rootedness. Educing the example of St
Andrew as a searcher in the call narratives, Meehan regards
Religious Education as a critical tool in transforming the lives
students in their spiritual quest. She regards the new Junior Cycle
(second level) curriculum as one that places the student at the
centre and focuses on the importance of personal integration,
good relationships and participating positively with community
and society. In a second article on a new Religious Education
curriculum in the Republic of Ireland, in this case a first (primary)
level programme, Anne Hession, the principal author, resonating
with Meehan's work, speaks of 'openness with roots', a concept
which emerged from Anthony Bryk's[7] research concerning the
impact of Vatican II on Catholic secondary education in the USA.
Hession emphasises the importance of dialogue between theology
and education while navigating the design of the Religious
Education and its approach to religion. In insisting that the
Catholic approach, in contrast to a constructivist approach, views
religion as having its origins in a divine Truth revealed by God,
Hession is making a very significant point. She then goes on to
discuss specific issues in relation to the *Catholic Preschool and
Primary Religious Education Curriculum for Ireland* (2015) which
provides the curriculum framework for Catholic religious educa-
tion of young children in both the North of Ireland and the
Republic. The overarching aim of developing religiously literate
Catholics of the future constitutes an equally significant point.

Sean Whittle, in *Religious Education in Catholic Schools: Contemporary Challenges*, poses a challenge to Towey and Robinson in suggesting that one of the challenges facing Religious Education in Catholic schools is that, in effect, 'Religious Education has become part and parcel of the wider exam factory that characterises secondary education'. This is just one of five challenges posited by Whittle, the others being the ambiguous, in his view, of the relationship with catechesis and faith formation, the need for clarification of the aims of Catholic education, practical issue of curriculum time and appropriately qualified teachers and reforms and the need to study two religions. While highlighted potential issues faced by Catholic schools in terms of the first four challenges, Whittle sees the requirement to study two religions as an opportunity for Catholic schools which often include students and indeed staff from a range of faith and cultural backgrounds, resonating with points made by Lucas, Towey and Robinson in their chapters.

Heads of Religious Education departments or RE-Co-ordinators will always be responsible, primarily, for the adoption, implementation and development of new curricula. Sarah Nash in *The Role of RE Co-ordinators in Primary Schools in England* steers the reader through the landscape of the role as subject leader, as a ministry and in relation to the leadership of the school, advocating strongly the centrality of Religious Education in the life of any school. Nash is very clear about the importance of the way in which the role is viewed by leadership, particularly in regard to the strong signal this sends to the staff, parents and the local and Deanery clergy. Modelling ministry on that of Christ features prominently in this chapter alongside the necessity for the RE Co-ordinator to have an input into the strategic leadership of a Catholic school min an endeavour to maintain its distinctive identity. In this latter context Teresa Lucas' chapter entitled *Chaplaincy and Religious Diversity* is of particular importance. Speaking from a position of strength as an experienced chaplain in a religiously diverse school, Lucas cites key ecclesial documents in balancing the tension between proclamation and dialogue which features strongly in this chapter. In citing the term 58 times, Lucas' retrieval of dialogue is rooted in two documents promulgated by the Pontifical Council for Inter-Religious Dialogue. In describing the maintenance of the balance between proclamation and dialogue as a challenge and an opportunity Lucas articulates a series of examples based on experience and worthy of serious reflection.

The third part of this volume focuses on leadership and governance. Professor Grace, in Catholic Schools' Self-Evaluation: Five International Challenges, identifies two distinctive forms of evaluation: Performative Secular Evaluation (PSEV) and Mission Catholic Evaluation (MCEV), analogous to the Section 5 and Section 48 inspections which take place in England. Focusing especially on MCEV, Grace proceeds to posit five challenges incorporating spirituality, mission integrity, commitment to the common good, Catholic school leadership and ethos. Grace concludes by suggesting that failure to take MCEV seriously could result in 'mission drift and the gradual cultural and educational incorporation of Catholic schools into State mandated educational regimes'. The inclusion of key definitions of mission drift and spiritual capital alongside Grace's distillation of a rich heritage of scholarship makes this chapter an essential read for Catholic leaders internationally.

In Challenges Facing Catholic Secondary Headteachers in a Contemporary Context, Simon Uttley takes a broad perspective and includes an all-pervading performativity and the introduction of British values into the educational hinterland as two of the key contemporary challenges. Uttley laments England's lowly place in international comparative studies on child well-being in spite of an august range of education policies enacted, presumably, with the promotion of human flourishing in mind. In an impressive blend of poetry, philosophy and scholarship, Uttley uses the Benthamite term 'panopticon' for the Ofsted inspection regime, evoking the image of an all-pervading system focusing essentially on measurable outcomes and their tracking which has the potential to challenge the holistic perspective canonised in Catholic tradition. Uttley goes on to address an array of challenges and argues persuasively that the 21st century Catholic Headteacher should model a pioneering counter-cultural approach whence 'educare is transfigured to educere[8], when education-as-moulding becomes education as a "leading out"; as epiphany'.

Turning from school leadership to governance Christopher Storr in *Trusteeship and Governance of Catholic Schools* argues convincingly that there is an urgent need for governors to experience formation in Catholic ethos and mission analogous to the training experienced by many governors around legal and managerial issues. Storr cites statistical evidence relating to student admissions and teacher appointments alongside an increasing marketisation in support of his claim that Catholic identity is in danger of being eroded. Storr makes it clear that his is a development of Gerald Grace's work which, in essence, argues that measurable outcomes has exercised a hegemony over the concepts of human dignity and indeed human flourishing with the focus on a divine destiny being rendered nebulous by an over-emphasis on utility. Citing authoritative Church documents in support of his discussion Storr concludes by suggesting that

> there needs to be a redoubling of effort by trustees to promote the Catholic perspective for governors, and that they should recognise more fully than they appear to at the moment the decisive role that governors can play in the evangelising work of the church.

In a final chapter in this section on leadership John Lydon discusses the increasing focus on the formation of Catholic school leadership within the Catholic Church through the prism of one Masters programme, the MA in Catholic School Leadership at St Mary's University, London. After a brief introduction outlining the provenance of the programme, Lydon discusses the nature of the programme, to highlight its demonstrable focus on formation and to underline contemporary challenges. Critical scholarship and authoritative Church pronouncements are retrieved in support of the programme's claim that the primary challenge for all Catholic school leaders is to maintain a balance between school improvement issues and Catholic distinctiveness. In relation to the person of the teacher it could be claimed that there should be an equally germane balance between vocation and profession, both viewed as aspects of discipleship. Lydon concludes by documenting a new innovation created by him which addresses the formation of aspiring early career leaders, recognised as such by their Headteachers. This is proving popular in the new era of academisation when responsibility for formation is increasingly in the hands of the directors of the multi-academy trusts.

In concluding this introductory chapter the editor is confident in suggesting that this book is of interest to a wide range of constituencies within the world of Catholic education, ranging from colleagues involved in initial teacher education to those involved in lifelong learning encompassing context, Religious Education and leadership. It is of particular interest to Catholic school leaders who are faced by the challenges articulated in the various chapters, be they around maintaining a strong Catholic identity in general or specific issues in relation to the provision for Religious Education and chaplaincy or the ever-increasing range of reforms around the governance and management of schools. In this latter context, the book will also be invaluable to school governors and religious trustees. Finally, it is hoped that this new book will go beyond that of its predecessor and be the standard textbook for more than one Masters programme across the world of Catholic education!

Acknowledgements

As editor, I would like to express my gratitude to all the authors who contributed chapters to this volume as it relies to a large extent on their work. The names of individual authors are to be found at the beginning of each chapter. The particular reflections on aspects of education and policy in different countries have been important and fascinating in their own right—but also have illuminative impacts as a generalisable set of phenomena for Catholic education internationally. Initially the project was directed jointly by myself and the late Rev. Professor Michael Hayes, whose earlier *Contemporary Catholic Education* (2002) co-edited with Dr Liam Gearon is the antecedent to this latest volume. My debt to him for both his intellectual critique, encouragement and leadership is immense.

Throughout putting this work together, I was able to rely on critical scholarly inputs from my UK, Irish and American colleagues at meetings in London and Limerick. My indebtedness to them for their intellectual stimulation, collegial support and enjoyable scholarly camaraderie. I have also had the benefit of critical insights from colleagues at conferences in the UK, United States and Rome which have enabled the experience of different countries, cultures and school systems to be included in this volume.

Over the period of four years, I have depended on quite a significant amount of highly skilled research, editorial, administrative expertise and assistance to sustain this work. Special thanks to Professor Gerald Grace at the Centre for Research and Development in Catholic Education (CDRCE), St Mary's London for providing a collegial and inspirational research environment. My warm thanks also to Dr Caroline Healy, Senior Lecturer, MA Catholic School Leadership and Kathryn Penny, administrator at St Mary's University, London. They both kindly stepped in to support my editorial duties to bring this book to fruition following the untimely death of Rev. Professor Michael Hayes. I also wish to thank Orla Banks at Mary Immaculate College, University of Limerick for administrative support in the initial stages of the work. Finally, I would like to acknowledge Rev. Dr Paul Haffner, the Theological and Editorial Director at Gracewing Publishing for his tremendous support and guidance during this long process.

Dr John Lydon, KC*HS (Editor)
St Mary's University, London
1 March 2018

Notes

[1]   Congregation for Catholic Education, *Educating Today and Tomorrow* (2014), II.

[2]   M. A. Hayes & L. Gearon (eds), *Contemporary Catholic Education* (Leominster: Gracewing, 2002).

[3]   J. Arthur, 'The De-Catholicising of the Curriculum in English Catholic Schools'. In: G. Grace, *International Studies in Catholic Education* Vol. 5/No. 1 (2013), 83.

[4]   Pope Francis, Apostolic Exhortation *Evangelii Gaudium* (2013), 42.

[5]   Pope Francis, *Homily for the Solemnity of Ss Peter and Paul* (29 June 2015).

[6]   Congregation for Catholic Education, *The Religious Dimension of Education in a Catholic School* (1988), 66.

[7]   A. S. Bryk, P. B. Holland & V. E. Lee, *Catholic Schools and the Common Good* (Cambridge MA: Harvard University Press, 1993).

[8]   M. Craft, 'Education for Diversity'. In: M. Craft (ed.), *Education and Cultural Pluralism* (London & Philadelphia: Falmer Press, 1984), 5–26.

I CONTEXT

1 CATHOLIC SECONDARY EDUCATION IN THE IRISH CONTEXT

Martin Browne OSB

Martin Browne OSB is a monk of Glenstal Abbey, County Limerick in Ireland, and is a former Headmaster of the abbey school. He is a member of the International Commission on Benedictine Education.

Introduction

THE WORDS OF Pope Francis, addressed to 'all Christians, everywhere, at this very moment', inviting them to a 'renewed personal encounter with Jesus Christ, or at least an openness to letting him encounter them'[1] offer a particular challenge to those engaged in the work of Catholic education. It is a challenge in the first place to deepen their own Christian lives, and thereby facilitate—or at least not obstruct—such personal encounters for those whom they serve in their schools and colleges.

That this is a two-fold task—personal and professional—is especially important in the case of work with young people, whose antennae for inauthenticity and cant are especially acute. Blessed Paul VI made this point as early as 1975: 'modern man listens more willingly to witnesses than to teachers, and if he does listen to teachers, it is because they are witnesses'[2] Pope Francis echoed this point when addressing new archbishops from around the world in June 2015. He could just as easily have been speaking to Catholic educators.

> Today there is no great need for masters, but for courageous witnesses, who are convinced and convincing...the most effective and authentic witness is one that does not contradict, by behaviour and lifestyle, what is preached with the word and taught to others! Teach prayer by praying, announce the faith by believing; offer witness by living![3]

From the time of the Second Vatican Council, the Church's Magisterium has provided much fine material to inspire and inform those who work in Catholic schools and colleges. Fine as these resources may be for the Church worldwide, every school and every student will always be inseparable from the particular context and culture in which they exist. Therefore any theological thinking about them which is worthy of the name needs, as a now classic text suggests, to take account of 'the spirit and message of the gospel; the tradition of the Christian people; the culture in which one is theologising; and social change in that culture'.[4] This chapter will attempt to analyse the second-level education sector in the Republic of Ireland in this way and identify some areas for further exploration.

Structural and Legislative Background

In common with many European countries, most Catholic second-level schools in Ireland form part of the public state-funded education system. Of the 711 second-level schools in the country, 335 are Catholic 'voluntary secondary schools' and nine are Catholic 'comprehensive schools'. Catholic bodies are also involved in trusteeship and management of many 'community schools' and 'community colleges'.[5] The term 'voluntary' may require some explanation outside Ireland. It is used to describe schools and other bodies, including hospitals, which though not owned by the state exist to provide a public benefit rather than as a commercial business. The vast majority of Catholic voluntary secondary schools in Ireland do not charge fees and rely on the state for almost all of their funding.

Most Catholic voluntary secondary schools were founded either by dioceses or by religious orders or congregations. Clergy and religious made up the core of their teaching staffs for many years and since the introduction of free education procedures for the management of Catholic voluntary secondary schools gave trustees the right to nominate clerics or religious directly to school posts, including principalship, without open competition. However, the Department of Education and Skills indicated in December 2017 that this right is to be scrapped. Unsurprisingly, the sharp decline in the numbers of clergy and religious personnel over the past forty years has brought significant change in this sector. Some schools closed, or were merged into community schools. Of the 335 that remain, many have few if any sisters, brothers or priests on staff. As the numbers of religious personnel declined further, many congregations transferred legal ownership of their schools to new trust bodies. Almost 75% of Catholic voluntary secondary schools now belong to trust bodies such as CEIST (Catholic Education an Irish Schools Trust), Le Chéile—A Catholic Schools Trust, and ERST (Edmund Rice Schools Trust).[6] These relatively new trust bodies all have very clear charters and other defining statements, declaring their schools to be Catholic, as do the schools which continue under the direct management of religious congregations and dioceses. What is less clear is what this designation actually means in the schools in question, and how it is understood and shared—or not—by the staff, students and parents concerned.

The legislative basis for the state's regulation of education in Ireland is the Education Act of 1998. The Act makes repeated reference to the 'characteristic spirit' of schools [emphasis added]:

- Section 9(d) of the Act requires schools to 'promote the moral, spiritual, social and personal development of students and provide health education for them, in consultation with their parents, *having regard to the characteristic spirit* of the school'.

- Section 15(2)(b) requires Boards of Management to 'uphold, and be accountable to the patron for so *upholding, the characteristic spirit of the school* as determined by the cultural, educational, moral, religious, social, linguistic and spiritual values and traditions which inform and are characteristic of the objectives and conduct of the school'.

- Section 15(2)(d) requires boards to publish 'the policy of the school concerning admission to and participation in the school, including the policy of the school relating to the expulsion and suspension of students and admission to and participation by students with disabilities or who have other special educational needs, and ensure that as regards that policy principles of equality and the right of parents to send their children to a school of the parents' choice are respected and such directions as may be made from time to time by the Minister, *having regard to the characteristic spirit* of the school and the constitutional rights of all persons concerned, are complied with'. Section 29 provides the right of appeal to the Department of Education and Skills (DES) in the event of a student not being enrolled by its school of choice.

- Section 30 gives the Minister for Education and Skills the authority to prescribe the curriculum and syllabus for schools. In doing this, the minister is required under Section 30(2)(b) to '*have regard to the characteristic spirit* of a school or class of school'. Section 30(2)(d) requires the minister to ensure that the time prescribed for each subject be such as 'to allow for such reasonable instruction time, as the board with the consent of the patron determines, for *subjects relating to or arising from the characteristic spirit* of the school'. This is the basis on which denominational schools, though state-funded, are entitled to develop denominationally-based Religious Education syllabi. This is balanced by the further provision that no student can be forced to attend instruction in a subject which is contrary to the conscience of his/her parents.

The framework established by the Education Act has been supplemented and amended by further legislation and regulation since then, most notably the Education (Welfare) Act 2000, Education for Persons with Special Educational Needs Act 2004, Education (Miscellaneous Provisions) Act 2007 and the Education (Amendment) Act 2012. The Education (Admissions to

Schools) Bill 2016, currently before the legislature, adds a significant level of regulation and restriction to the ways by which schools select their students. The Employment Equality Act 1998 and the Equal Status Act 2000 are also of significance for schools. Section 37(1) of the 1998 Act exempted a religious or educational institution from being found to have discriminated if it gives preference to an employee or prospective employee on religious grounds, or if it 'takes action which is reasonably necessary to prevent an employee or a prospective employee from undermining the religious ethos of the institution'. This exemption was removed by the Equality (Miscellaneous Provisions) Act 2015.

To summarise: Catholic schools in Ireland are, for the most part, state-funded, and so are subject to most of the same regulation and inspection as purely secular state schools. Curriculum and syllabus have until recently largely been prescribed by central government, although the new Junior Cycle Student Award currently being rolled out in the nation's schools gives more freedom to individual schools and teachers. Schools have limited discretion regarding enrolment and the individuals or groups whom they may prioritise. Similarly, a school which gives priority to a committed Catholic candidate above another when recruiting teachers will soon have no legal protection—even in the appointment of teachers of Religious Education. Unlike many other countries, the Church does not engage in its own separate regulation, inspection or accreditation of Catholic schools. A school is defined as Catholic solely by virtue of having a Catholic patron.

Teaching in a Catholic School

The Second Vatican Council declared that the proper function of a Catholic school is to 'to generate a community climate in the school that is permeated by the Gospel spirit of freedom and love' and 'to guide the adolescents in such a way that personality development goes hand in hand with the development of the 'new creature' that each one has become through baptism. It tries to relate all of human culture to the good news of salvation so that the light of faith will illumine everything that the students will gradually come to learn about the world, about life, and about the human person'.[7] The Council's teaching on the distinctive marks of Catholic education can be summarised as a) the educational climate, b) the personal development of each student, c) the relationship established between culture and the Gospel, d) the illumination of all knowledge with the light of faith.[8] In the Irish educational environment of today, operating schools in line with all four of these characteristics requires sensitivity and creativity on the part of patrons and trusts.

Church documents and papal teachings tend to presume that teachers in Catholic schools share this understanding of their mission. This is not a safe presumption to make in the case of Irish schools. Because the second-level education system in Ireland is so uniform, from a teacher's point of view, there is little difference between teaching Maths or English in a Catholic school and teaching Maths or English in another school. All second-level teachers are required to have a degree and a postgraduate qualification in Education, (or an integrated teaching degree) in order to be registered by the Teaching Council. Nothing further is required of teachers in Catholic schools and so jobseekers tend to apply for jobs in all sectors, frequently moving freely between sectors over the course of their career. That a particular school happens to be a Catholic school can often be a matter of indifference for the job-seeking teacher and employment equality legislation makes it difficult for interview panels to find out much about a prospective employee's faith commitment unless that information is volunteered by the candidate.

Teaching as Ministry

For much of the twentieth century, Ireland had unnaturally high numbers of clergy and religious, and these were seen as the guarantors of the Catholic identity of their schools, long before terms like 'ethos' and 'characteristic spirit' began to be used. Like so many other areas of church life in Ireland, this abundance of 'professional' religious people prevented—or obviated any perceived need for—lay people becoming similarly engaged with fostering the identity of Catholic schools. This has heightened the impact of the collapse of religious vocations over the last forty years. While much attention has been given to the training of lay people to serve as teachers of Religious Education, and as chaplains and pastoral workers of various types, until very recently very little energy and resources have been put into forming Catholic teachers as such. However, it is clear that RE teachers and chaplains cannot be expected to carry a school's Catholic identity on their own.

Teachers in Ireland in recent years have been forced to take on many new responsibilities apart from their core classroom work. Cutbacks in government funding have obliged mainstream teachers to take on tasks which would ordinarily be done by guidance counsellors, special education teachers and other specialists. It would be a mistake to think that a Catholic teacher's responsibility for fostering a school's Catholic identity is of a similar order. Cutbacks in public spending and 'cutbacks' in the numbers of religious and clergy in schools are not the same thing. As an important Vatican document reminds us, the most basic reason for the evolving role of Catholic laity in fostering the identity of Catholic schools is not merely a response to the decline in religious vocations, but is *theological*-based on the distinctive vocation of the lay faithful.[9]

The Dogmatic Constitution on the Church underlines the dignity of all the baptised:

> Therefore, the chosen People of God is one ... sharing a common dignity as members from their regeneration in Christ, having the same filial grace and the same vocation to perfection; possessing in common one salvation, one hope and one undivided charity...all share a true equality

with regard to the dignity and to the activity common to
all the faithful for the building up of the Body of Christ.[10]

Yet, it also emphasises the obligations that come with this, saying
that each member of the lay faithful 'must stand before the world
as a witness to the resurrection and life of the Lord Jesus and a
symbol of the living God'.[11] The Congregation for Catholic
Education has spelled this out even further for educators: 'The
life of the Catholic teacher must be marked by the exercise of a
personal vocation in the Church, and not simply by the exercise
of a profession'.[12] Such a vision of their work as a key element of
the noble vocation of all the Christian faithful has not been widely
appropriated by teachers in Catholic schools in Ireland, particularly by the majority who teach so-called 'secular' subjects.

Given the centralised and restricted educational environment
which I describe above, this chapter could appear to be a
dispiriting jeremiad. That is not the intention. While not too
many teachers may be quoting the documents of Vatican II with
reference to their work, much positive work has been and is being
done in the area of teacher formation and induction. Developments such as the consolidation of schools into the trusts
mentioned above and the work of education offices within
individual dioceses and religious congregations have enabled
schools to draw on specialists in leadership, ethos and faith
development as they seek to nurture their Catholic ethos. How
long these resources can be maintained without provision being
made for the funding of trusteeship is, however, a pressing
question.[13] Also, interesting new resources are being produced
to support school leaders in promoting spiritual reflection among
their colleagues.[14] To borrow a phrase coined by Gerald Grace
in the English context, the 'spiritual capital' of Catholic schools
is being developed in new ways.[15]

The fact that most teachers in Catholic schools may have little
or no sense of having an ecclesial vocation does not mean that
they are incapable of developing such a sense or that they are
necessarily unwilling to be invited along such a road. It is often

the case that this view of their role has simply never been put to them—a by-product, perhaps, of there not being any specific formation requirement for teaching in Catholic schools. One teacher has accurately described the problem: 'this role is not being communicated to them; perhaps because of management's fear of litigation or hostility or perhaps management are not quite sure how to go about broaching the subject'.[16]

If Catholic school leaders are serious about their own roles, then they need to overcome this kind of fear and embarrassment. My own limited experience of introducing prayer, or the discussion of ethos, or exploration of the Benedictine tradition during staff meetings (at a Benedictine school) was often tinged with nervousness and a certain embarrassment about asking colleagues to—in Alastair Campbell's phrase—'do God'. My embarrassment was generally misplaced. Colleagues, even those who made no secret of their disconnection from the institutional church, were almost always open to a vision of God, to experiences of prayer, and to learning more about the particular spiritual tradition in which the school stood. Most were interested in the values which the school sought to promote and many could see links between these values and their own professional practice.

Conclusion

Catholic schools in Ireland have had students from other Christian denomination and other faiths for a long time. The numbers have increased greatly over the past twenty years. Furthermore, as Irish society becomes increasingly secular, Catholic schools now have growing numbers of students from families who are only nominally Christian or who have no faith commitment at all. All of this has brought questions of pluralism and inclusiveness to the fore. Catholic schools rightly wish to be inclusive, but this does not mean the dilution of their specifically Catholic ethos. As guidelines circulated to voluntary secondary schools in 2010 put it: 'before we can comfortably host students of other faiths and their needs, it seems necessary that we address our own identity as Catholic schools and how we approach the responsibilities we have towards the faith development of Catholic students'.[17]

Balance is not always easy to achieve. Catholic schools should be unashamedly and proudly Catholic, but not hothouses of indoctrination or proselytism. Catholic schools need to have teachers who uphold and support their ethos and teachers who have a vocational sense of being Catholic educators, yet they should not be closed shops where the gifts of teachers with different beliefs aren't welcome. They need to have a big and expansive sense of the Gospel and the human person, yet they also need to communicate the teachings of the Church faithfully.

What might be the principal theological task for a school trustee or leader in Ireland today? I would suggest that it is the task of *translation*—of re-visiting the mission or characteristic spirit of their school, laying hold of it afresh and seeking ways of expressing it which speak not only to students and their families, but to the teachers who work in the school too, thus facilitating them in living out their baptismal vocation. Translation 'serves the purpose of seeking to make a text come alive so that it can be internalised, owned and acted upon by a new target group'.[18] This task of translation is part of what has become known as the 'New Evangelisation'—re-proposing the Gospel, encounter with Christ and participation in the life of the Church to those who may have become distant. Cardinal Donald Wuerl has identified three stages in this task: 'the renewal or deepening of our faith intellectually and affectively; a new confidence in the truth of our faith; and a willingness to share it with others'.[19]

Confidence is an important characteristic to underline in this regard, particularly in Ireland, where the toxic legacy of the revelations of ministerial abuse of children has made some church voices timid. Speaking to leaders and managers of voluntary secondary schools in 2015, the then Chairman of the Catholic Schools Partnership, Fr Michael Drumm, essayed such a confident translation of the ethos of Catholic education:

It seeks to bring the worlds of knowledge and culture into dialogue with what was revealed in the person of Jesus Christ so that the free choice for religious belief is not an irrational withdrawal from science and culture but an embrace of a holistic understanding of the human person. This is why the word 'and' is very important in understanding Catholicism: faith *and* reason, scripture *and* tradition, grace *and* nature, religion and culture, belief *and* science...There are few more important tasks facing Catholic education today that to retrieve this blessed 'and'. Failure to do so can isolate believers in an intellectual ghetto.[20]

Notes

[1] Pope Francis, Apostolic Exhortation *Evangelii Gaudium* (2013), 3.

[2] Pope Paul VI, Apostolic Exhortation *Evangelii Nuntiandi* (1975).

[3] Pope Francis, *Homily for the Solemnity of Ss Peter and Paul* (29 June 2015).

[4] S. B. Bevans, *Models of Contextual Theology* (Maryknoll, NY: Orbis Books, 2002), 1.

[5] Department of Education and Skills, Ireland *Data on Individual Schools 2016/17*, available at https://www.education.ie/en/Publications/ Statistics/Data-on-Individual-Schools/ (accessed 11 January 2018).

[6] Catholic Education—an Irish Schools Trust (CEIST): www.ceist.ie; Le Chéile—a Catholic Schools Trust: www.lecheiletrust.ie and Edmund Rice Schools Trust (ERST): www.erst.ie, respectively.

[7] Vatican II, *Gravissimum Educationis* - Declaration on Christian Education (1965), 8.

[8] Congregation for Catholic Education, *The Religious Dimension of Education in a Catholic School* (1988), 1.

[9] Congregation for Catholic Education, *Lay Catholics in Schools: Witnesses to Faith* (1982) 2 and Vatican II, Lumen Gentium - Dogmatic Constitution on the Church and Decree on the Apostolate of the Laity (1964).

[10] Vatican II, *Lumen Gentium* (1964), 32.

[11] *Ibid.*, 38.

[12] Congregation for Catholic Education, *Lay Catholics in Schools: Witnesses to Faith* (1982), 37.

[13] See M. Darmody & E. Smyth, 'Governance and Funding of Voluntary Secondary Schools'. In: *Ireland Research Series* (Dublin: ESRI, 2013), No. 34, Ch. 4.

[14] See especially A. Meehan, *Joining the Dots: A Programme of Spiritual Reflection and Renewal for Educators* (Dublin: Veritas, 2012).

[15] G. Grace, *Catholic Schools: Mission, Markets and Morality* (Abingdon: Routledge-Falmer, 2002), 236–240.

[16] M. O'Sullivan, '*Nemo dat quod non habet: Towards a Further Understanding of the Role of the Lay Teacher of Non-Religious Subjects in an Irish Post-Primary Catholic School*' (Unpublished MA thesis, Mary Immaculate College, University of Limerick, 2012), 6.4.

[17] Association of Management of Catholic Secondary Schools, *Guidelines on the Inclusion of Students of Other Faiths in Catholic Secondary Schools* (2010), 6.

[18] J. Sullivan, 'Catholic education as ongoing translation'. In: *International Studies in Catholic Education*, Vol. 4/No. 2 (2012), 201–207.

[19] D. Wuerl, 'What Catholic schools can do to advance the cause of the New Evangelisation in the world'. In: *International Studies in Catholic Education*, Vol. 5/No. 2 (2013), 129.

[20] M. Drumm, Address at JMB/AMCSS (Joint Managerial Body/Association of Management of Catholic Secondary Schools) Annual Conference, Killarney (29 April 2015).

2 A BALKANIZED EDUCATIONAL LANDSCAPE: PUBLIC, CHARTER, AND CATHOLIC SCHOOLS IN THE UNITED STATES

Fr Ronald J. Nuzzi

Ronald Nuzzi is a priest of the Diocese of Youngstown, Ohio in the United States and currently serves on the faculty of the Alliance for Catholic Education (ACE) at the University of Notre Dame in South Bend, Indiana.

Introduction

THE PROVISION OF educational opportunities for children in the United States is currently undergoing significant modification and development. For the past several centuries, the educational landscape has been clearly dominated by two distinct sectors: public schools, educating nearly ninety percent (90%) of all students; and private or sectarian schools, often religiously affiliated, serving approximately ten percent (10%) of all students.[1] In recent decades, however, free market forces, legislative changes, and an overall climate of increased accountability among educators, parents, and political leaders have initiated some disruptive innovation into the once stable system.

Catholic schools have traditionally comprised the largest part of the private school sector, with over 6,500 schools serving nearly two million students in 2013–2014. However, the Catholic school market share has been on a steady decline since at least 1964–1965, when Catholic schools numbered 13,000 across the US and served 5.6 million students.[2] Many factors contributed to this marked decline: the increasing secularization of society; the absence of vowed religious women and men to staff the schools at low or no cost; skyrocketing financial needs for technology, employment benefits, and facilities; and new competition for students in the form of charter schools.

Charter schools are public schools in as much as they are funded in the same way as traditional public schools, which is through local property taxes. They are different from the typical public school in that they are independent schools of choice that are exempt from many of the regulatory and often bureaucratic mandates often found in public schools. The 'charter' itself is a binding legal agreement wherein the school operators agree to specific accountability measures for academic achievement, financial sustainability, and community and parental involvement in exchange for more degrees of freedom to structure the curriculum, calendar, and pedagogical approaches in ways designed to maximize student growth.[3] The resulting educational ethos is often one with a more focused vision and mission than traditional public schools, in large part inspired by the highly motivated parents who choose such schools for their children, a lower teacher/student ratio, a heightened experience of community in the school and with parents, and the introduction of curricular and extra-curricular innovations.

Using Catholic schools as a proxy for understanding the private school sector, this analysis is intended to explain the differences in the public, charter, and Catholic schools in the US by shedding light on various innovative developments in education, with a view to illustrating how current trends are collapsing the commonly held public/private school categories. Four themes are discussed: 1) funding differences among public, charter, and Catholic schools; 2) the general contours of the educational reform movement in the US; 3) the multiple meanings of choice; and resulting from these three, 4) the blurring, even collapsing of the public/private distinction in US schools.

Funding Across the Sectors

Traditional public schools receive their funding from property taxes paid by every home, business, and land owner. Monies are collected locally and then distributed to the schools, with most school districts relying on a formula that translates collected tax dollars into per pupil expenditures for each student. Because property values vary widely from urban to suburban to rural districts, revenues available to fund schools are not equally available to all students or to all schools. Districts with high property values and therefore high tax revenues tend to have schools that are better resourced. Rural areas, often less popu-lated, and high poverty areas in many urban environments, do not generate nearly as much property tax revenue as suburban locations. This situation often results in students with multiple disadvantages attending schools with the least resources.

For example, recent spending per pupil in the state of New York totalled $19,076 in 2011. Close behind New York stood the District of Columbia (Washington, DC) at $18,475. The top five also included the state of Alaska ($16,674), the state of New Jersey ($15,968), and the state of Vermont ($15,925). At the other end of the spectrum, available revenue from property taxes did not generate nearly the equivalent funds to operate schools. The bottom five states in terms of per pupil expenses in 2011 were: Mississippi ($7,928), Arizona ($7,666), Oklahoma ($7,587), Idaho ($6,824), and Utah ($6,212). Moreover, within state discrepancies are often more pronounced than between state differences. For example, within the state of Ohio, Shaker Heights, a tony suburb of the city of Cleveland spent $16,756 per pupil in 2011 while Butler County schools in the southwestern corner of the same state spent $4,616.[4] Because of these huge disparities in funding, the quality of educational programming-from teachers' salaries and facilities to technology and science laboratories-vary radically among states and within districts, resulting in what one author has termed 'savage inequalities'.[5] Recent research has suggested that such an imbalanced system is grossly unjust, locking large groups of people into their social class of birth origin, rather than education itself being a path to upward social mobility.[6] Such a 'hereditary meritocracy' results in the dominant class behaving in ways to protect their dominance, learning self-preservation through the inheritance of privilege.

Catholic and private schools, on the other hand, are tuition-driven institutions, with parents paying large sums in addition to their property taxes to fund the cost of their children's education outside of the public school. Selected often for religious reasons, these schools are also characterized by high academic standards for all students, discipline, strong parent relationships, an emphasis on moral education and character formation, and social and cultural immersion into the religious beliefs and traditions of the sponsoring faith denomination. In the Catholic sector, the average elementary school tuition was $3,673 in 2013; the average secondary tuition was $9,622.[7] Although Catholic school tuition also varies across the nation and within dioceses from parish to parish, the differences are not typically as large as found among public schools.[8]

Charter schools present themselves as a bit of a hybrid, occupying a space on the educational landscape that has qualities of both public and private schools. Charter schools are public schools and receive full government funding. However, because of the freedom they enjoy by law, they are able to innovate and adapt quickly, revise curriculum, hire new staff, and maintain an entrepreneurial spirit in the overall administration of the school. Typical charter school adaptations include: a longer school day, student uniforms, before- and after-care programs, character education, and student leadership development. Indeed, some scholars have observed that the best charter schools resemble Catholic schools in conduct and affect, albeit without mention of religion. Because charter schools are public schools, they are precluded from charging tuition. The result of this policy presents a serious challenge to many Catholic schools in urban areas, where students have left the Catholic school for the charter school, hoping to find a similar though not identical educational environment at no cost.[9]

The Educational Reform Movement

In direct response to the inherent inequalities of the public educational system in the US, many efforts have been undertaken to improve educational outcomes for all students and to address the demographic stratification of the American school system, especially as it involves racial segregation.[10] This educational reform movement has been focused on equality of educational opportunity for all students. Using charter school legislation and other policy initiatives, educational reformers are seeking to challenge the monopoly of the traditional public schools, wrestle decision-making power from the omnipresent teacher unions, empower parents to have meaningful options in the education of their children, and thereby expand the availability and accessibility of good schools to all children, especially those without good educational options currently.[11] As the system is structured today, 'demography is destiny'.[12] Middle class and upper middle class families settle in the suburbs, purchasing homes and thereby buying into a property tax structure that supports a high quality education, with modern facilities and well compensated professional staff. Catholic, private, and religiously affiliated schools are also viable options. Poor families, recent immigrants, racial and ethnic minorities, and those sociologists have come to call the 'working poor'[13] on the other hand, cluster in urban centres and have limited access to high quality schools, facilities, or staff.

A singularly important construct in the educational reform movement is the notion of choice, understood as the empowerment of parents to select that school or educational environment that best fits their family's needs. This empowerment of parents to exercise such discretion requires major changes in educational policy and legislation, for if a parent's choice is to be real and meaningful, it must be supported by funding. Absent such legitimate parental choice, children of families in poverty in the urban core have but one educational option available to them—the local public school. With fully funded parental choice, such children could attend any school—public, private, Catholic, or, charter—of their parent's choosing.

Choice and its Multiple Meanings

Educational choice has taken on many forms in recent years, responding to the multiple needs of families and in response to local, state, and federal legislative changes. Ten distinct types of choice programs have emerged in recent years, all sharing the same aim of creating equality of educational opportunity by empowering parents to identify and select the best schools and educational options for their children. Among these types of education choice are: charter schools; virtual schools; public school choice; course choice, magnet schools; homeschooling; vouchers; individual tuition tax credits; scholarship tax credits; and education savings accounts.[14] The table following provides a brief explanation of each type of choice program, explaining how the program provides benefit to students by increasing the available options to parents.[15]

Choice programs are currently designed according to one of three sets of rubrics: means-tested programs; failing schools programs; and special needs scholarship programs. Means-tested programs target students from low income families, who qualify for choice based on household income. Failing schools programs are intended for students whose assigned public school is persistently of low academic quality. These programs support a parent's choice to provide a new educational opportunity in a different school, public or private. Special needs scholarship programs are designed specifically for students with special needs and fund their attendance at a public or private school that can best address their unique learning needs.

TYPES OF EDUCATIONAL CHOICE		
SCHOLARSHIP TAX CREDITS Scholarship tax credits programs give families greater access to high-quality private schools by providing incentives for businesses and individuals to get involved in education reform. In these programs, companies and individuals receive tax credits for donating to nonprofit organizations that provide scholarships to students.	**SCHOOL VOUCHERS** Voucher programs give children (usually children from low-income families, children in failing schools, or children with special needs) greater access to high-quality private schools. In voucher programs, educational dollars "follow the child" and parents select private schools and receive state-funded scholarships to pay tuition.	**CHARTER SCHOOLS** Charter schools are public schools run by educators, members of the community, or other bodies, using innovative and specialized education programs. These schools have a fair amount of autonomy and operate without the bureaucracy that often plagues traditional public schools.
EDUCATION SAVINGS ACCOUNTS Education savings account programs give parents the power to use their child's state education dollars on a variety of educational options, including tuition and fees, textbooks, and tutoring. In these programs, families receive a debit card with funds available for approved education expenses and are able to choose the best education for their children.	**HOMESCHOOLING** Homeschooling has long been an educational option for families across the country. With the growth of online education and full curriculum available to parents, homeschooling allows parents the option of tailoring their children's education at home.	**VIRTUAL SCHOOLS** Virtual, or online education allows students to take one or all school courses online, allowing for more flexibility and options in education. **PUBLIC SCHOOL CHOICE** Public school choice (also known as open enrollment) allows students attending poor-performing public schools to attend a higher-performing public school inside or outside the student's assigned school district. Public school choice is an important option for students assigned to failing schools because of their ZIP code.
INDIVIDUAL TUITION TAX CREDITS Individual state income tax credits of significant size can be used for a child's educational expenses, including private school tuition, and can help families choose educational tools they otherwise could not afford.	**MAGNET SCHOOLS** Magnet schools are public schools that offer specific education programs, often emphasizing academic subjects like math, science, and technology, or use specific instructional approaches. **COURSE CHOICE** Course Choice allows K-12 students to enroll in individual course options, from both public and private providers, using state funds. Many of these courses are online but some are offered in traditional or blended learning formats.	

2013-2014 SCHOOL CHOICE YEAR BOOK

Educational choice of the types delineated above served over 300,000 students in 2013. During that time, there were 39 programs located in 18 states plus the District of Columbia. While this total is a small proportion of the nearly 55 million school age students in the US, the number of students participating in some form of choice program has been steadily increasing since 1990, and most researches see the trend continuing unabated for the foreseeable future.[16]

The Blurring of the Public/Private Distinction

Although it is early in the educational reform movement, the demonstrated success of choice programs thus far enables educational leaders, parents, and government agencies to envision a brighter future for US schools. High parental satisfaction with these programs has inspired political leaders of all stripes to support new legislation that funds some type of parental choice. Religious leaders have also been actively engaged in the political sphere, using their personal influence with local, state, and federal legislatures to highlight the struggles of low income families and to advocate on behalf of children trapped in poverty and in failing schools. As more and more public funds flow into choice programs, it becomes increasingly unclear which schools are public and which are private.

In a broad sense, since all schools educate children and thereby help shape, sustain, and preserve the social fabric of the republic, all schools serve a public purpose. However, until recently only public schools were eligible for funding. Choice programs alter that dynamic, finding legally and legislatively acceptable ways for public funds to support the education of children at private, even religious schools. As choice programs proliferate and succeed, it is likely that more and more tax dollars will flow into the private school market, expanding enrollments, and thereby shifting increasing percentages of the available student population from public schools into private ones. These market forces, it is hoped, will help in the overall improvement and renewal of all schools, forcing poor performing schools to improve or close.

In such an environment, the distinction between public and private schools may become increasingly moot. All schools do serve similar, though not identical, purposes. And if their funding stream is rooted in tax monies and their accountability measures are publicly mandated and shared, all schools may eventually be understood as public schools, that is, traditional public schools, charter public schools, Catholic public schools, and so forth. In such a scenario where educational choice was guaranteed and all educational options were publicly funded, quality of educational opportunity may finally be realized.

The educational reform movement is slowly levelling the playing field so that all schools can compete for students and funding on an equitable basis. In what has come to be known as 'the money follows the child,' reform advocates desire to place critical decisions into the hands of parents, expand their options beyond the immediate neighbourhood public school, fund all available options equally and fully, and then allow free market forces to fill the great schools and empty the bad ones. Catholic schools, struggling to compete with the tuition-free charter schools, would benefit greatly in such a system.

Research focused on sector effects in recent years has found many positive aspects of Catholic schools. While Catholic and other private schools have consistently fared well in academic measures when compared to public schools,[17] examination of the role Catholic schools play as community institutions is a new area of study. Focused on large, urban environments where public, private, and charter schools co-exist, recent studies have found positive and pro-social civic effects from the presence of Catholic schools that are not readily in evidence in other school sectors such as charter schools and public schools.[18] For example, Catholic school closures have been linked to increased crime and disorder in urban neighbourhoods and decreased social cohesion. Stated positively, the presence of a Catholic school helps stabilize a neighbourhood, increase the quality of life for all residents, and contributes to the common good. Charter schools, often characterized as the tuition-free alternative to Catholic schools, do not tend to result in reduced crime rates or increases in social cohesion in their neighbourhoods.

Conclusion

Gross inequalities in the funding of schools in the United States has created an educational system that is arguably unjust. Property taxes are the primary source of revenue for schools, with the result that some schools are well funded while others are not. Funding levels per pupil vary by up to fifty percent (50%) across a state. Students from wealthier homes and neighbourhoods have access to better schools than students from lower income homes and neighbourhoods. Rather than being a driver of upward social mobility and increasing educational attainments, public schools often sustain and perpetuate economically based social stratification.

An educational reform movement has begun in the United States, insisting on the primary role of parents in the education of their children and offering parents real and funded choices to select the school that best meets their children's needs. This choice takes on many forms, including within sector reforms such as charter schools and public school choice within a given district. More recently, it has also included novel approaches such as voucher, tax credits, and education savings accounts that create alternative ways to fund education by including all schools, public and private. Catholic schools in particular stand to benefit from these new legislative efforts. Having demonstrated high levels of success in academic and social measures, Catholic schools are increasingly the likely choice of parents who are fully empowered to select the best school for their children.

Notes

[1]   Council for American Private Education (CAPE), *Private Education: Good for Students, Good for Families, Good for America* (Germantown, MD: CAPE, 2014). The National Center for Education Statistics (NCES) a service of the US Department of Education in Washington, DC also collects relevant public and private school data. See *Private School Universe Survey: 1999–2000* (Washington, DC: NCES, 2001); *Private Schools: A Brief Portrait* (Washington, DC: NCES, 2002); *Projections of Education Statistics to 2013* (Washington, DC: NCES, 2003). A detailed précis is available at http://nces.ed.gov/fastfacts/display.asp?id=372 (Retrieved 1 February 2015).

2 National Catholic Educational Association (NCEA) *United States Catholic Elementary and Secondary Schools 2013-2014: The Annual Statistical Report on Schools, Enrollment and Staffing* (Washington, DC: NCEA, 2014).

3 D. McDonald, PVBM, 'Charter Schools'. In: T.C. Hunt, E.A. Joseph, and R. J. Nuzzi (eds), *Catholic Schools in the United States An Encyclopedia* (Westport, CT: Greenwood Press, 2004), 137–139.

4 StateImpact Ohio, *Ohio School District Expenditures*, available at http://stateimpact.npr.org/ohio/2012/01/17/see-how-much-each-ohio-school-district-spends-per-student/. Retrieved 1 February 2015. The Ohio General Assembly, also known as the state legislature, provides a searchable database at http://ode.legislature.state.oh.us/ (Retrieved 30 January 2015).

5 J. Kozol, *Savage Inequalities: Children in America's Schools* (New York: Crown Publishers, 1991).

6 *The Economist,* 'An Hereditary Meritocracy', 24-30 January 2015, Vol. 414/No. 8922, 17–20.

7 National Catholic Educational Association (NCEA) *United States Catholic Elementary and Secondary Schools 2013-2014: The Annual Statistical Report on Schools, Enrollment, and Staffing* (Washington, DC: NCEA, 2014). National Catholic school data can also be located online at NCEA's website. For regular updating, see http://ncea.org/data-information/catholic-school-data (Retrieved 22 January 2015).

8 J. C. Harris, *The Cost of Catholic Parishes and Schools* (Kansas City, MO: Sheed & Ward, 1996).

9 A. M. Lackman, 'The Collapse of Catholic School Enrollment: The Unintended Consequence of the Charter School Movement', *Albany Government Law Review*, Vol. 6 (25 February 2003), 2–20. For more discussion on the correlation between charter school growth in urban areas and Catholic school decline, see C. E. Finn, Jr. & A. Smarick, Editorial, *'Our Endangered Catholic Schools'*. In: *The Washington Post*, 21 April 2009, at A23 (citing Catholic schools as having a long track record of successfully educating ill-served populations); *'The Catholic School Crisis'*, *The New York Post*, 15 May 2006, at 28 (discussing the high performance of Catholic schools as compared to public schools among poor neighborhoods in New York City).

10 G. Miron, J. L. Ursche, W. J. Mathis & E. Tornquist, *Schools Without Diversity: Education Management Organizations, Charter Schools and the Demographic Stratification of the American School System* Education and the Public Interest Center (Boulder, CO: University of Colorado, 2010), 1–31.

11 J. F. Mead & P. C. Green III, *Using Charter School Legislation and Policy to Advance Equal Educational Opportunity* National Education Policy Center (Boulder, CO: University of Colorado, February 2012). Retrieved

1 February 2015 from http://nepc.colorado.edu/publication/chatering-equity.

[12] There has been much speculation in scholarly circles regarding the coining and first usage of this now popular phrase. For a recent analysis, see http://weekspopulation.blogspot.com/2013/11/the-origins-of-demography-is-destiny.html. Speculation ranges from an origin in France in the 1800s attributed to French philosopher Auguste Comte to a 1970 publication, *The Real Majority* by R. Scammon & B. Wattenberg (New York: Coward-McCann).

[13] D. K. Shipler, *The Working Poor: Invisible in America* (New York: Vintage Books, 2004).

[14] Alliance for School Choice, *School Choice Yearbook 2013-2014: Hope. Action. Results* (Washington, DC: Alliance for School Choice, 2014). See federal statistics at http://nces.ed.gov/fastfacts/display.asp?id=372.(Retrieved 11 January 2015).

[15] *Ibid.*, 9.

[16] *Ibid.*, Choice first emerged in 1990 with the first program in Milwaukee, Wisconsin, so the movement is but 25 years old.

[17] H. Braun, F. Jenkins & W. Grigg, *Comparing Private Schools and Public Schools Using Hierarchical Linear Modeling* US Department of Education (Washington, DC: NCES, 2006).

[18] M. F. Brinig & N. Stelle Garnett, 'Catholic Schools, Charter Schools and Urban Neighborhoods,' *University of Chicago Law Review*, Vol. 79/No. 1 (2012), 31.

3 RESEARCHING CATHOLIC EDUCATION

Dr Chris Richardson

Chris Richardson is a retired Catholic secondary headteacher and diocesan commissioner. He completed a doctoral thesis on the theological disposition of lay Catholic headteachers, and is currently an associate lecturer in Catholic school leadership at St Mary's University, Twickenham.

Introduction

THERE CONTINUES TO be a healthy interest in conducting research into Catholic education. At St Mary's University in Twickenham alone, around thirty people each year submit dissertations as part of their MA in Catholic school leadership. If asked, these researchers will almost certainly claim to be doing educational or social science research. Few if any will claim to be doing theology. This chapter explores an alternative approach to researching Catholic education. It draws on the theoretical perspective and experience of those engaged in empirical theological research, which involves a synthesis of theology and the empirical methods of social science.

Practical/Pastoral Theology

There are a number of ways of classifying theology but, for our purpose, I have taken a simple model that claims three main starting points for theology. One is the study of Scripture and requires methods borrowed from linguistics and linguistic sciences as well as archaeology and the history of religion. Another starting point is beliefs and doctrines. This is the domain of systematic theology, where the method is philosophical. Third, the starting point is experience and action, and recruits the methods of the social sciences. This latter is known as practical theology and it is under this umbrella that we locate empirical theological research.[1]

Catholic education is concerned with the synthesis of faith and life. Catholic schools and universities, to different degrees, are places where people experience a Christian community and learn to live out their faith amidst the complexity of everyday life. They offer a rich source of experience and action in a Catholic context for the practical theologian to explore.

Within Catholic circles practical theology has not enjoyed a significant following. In part this is because St Thomas Aquinas, who remains an enduring and influential source of theological inspiration, understood theology to be more speculative than practical. In part it is because Martin Luther regarded all theology as practical and consequently practical theology was seen as Protestant. Generally, Catholics have preferred the description 'pastoral theology' and this has mainly been taught in seminaries as part of the preparations of priests for their pastoral ministry.

Vatican II shifted the Church's focus from a God, who was somewhere else,[2] to a God, who is active in history and encouraged an openness of the Church to the world.[3] Responding to this, prominent Catholic theologians such as Karl Rahner[4] and David Tracey[5] endorsed practical theology. In the UK pastoral journals such as *The Pastoral Review* have encouraged a conversation between academics and practitioners. In his constitution of Catholic Universities, St. John Paul II supported the incorporation of secular methodology into the study of theology.[6] However, it is only recently that Catholic theologians have begun to make helpful contributions in the field of practical theology.[7]

Empirical Theological Research

Empirical theological research does not study God but rather uses the empirical methods of social science to explore the characteristics of a faith community such as the attitudes, beliefs and practices of those involved in Catholic education.[8] After all, the social and educational world, the world of human experience, 'speaks of the creative power of God' as much as the natural world does.[9] In the action of believers God's saving grace is revealed.[10] Empirical theology applies the methods already associated with investigating human experience to those aspects of theology, which lend themselves to such an approach. It is not concerned with abstract ideas but with concrete situations and the particular experiences of individuals. This is often the experience of those researching Catholic education.

A number of different ways of making use of empirical methods to study theology have developed. In the UK its influence can be seen in the 'pastoral cycle' of 'experience, explore, reflect, respond,' that has been used in many formation sessions in diocese and parishes.[11] Theological Action Research has also been developed by the Action Research—Church and Society (ARCS) project established at Heythrop College in London in 2002.[12] Leslie Francis and William Kay have been instrumental in developing what has become known as 'empirical theology' although much of the theoretical perspective and terminology has been developed by Hans van der Ven in the Netherlands.[13] This latter approach has been used widely in educational settings. A number of characteristics are common to these approaches although they do not share them all with the same intensity. It is these characteristics which can be used to shape theological research into Catholic education.

Characteristics of an Empirical Theological Approach

1. Paying Attention to the Theology of the Ordinary Christian

We tend to think of theology as something done by academics or ordained ministers. Indeed, across the centuries theologians have considered it to be a science. According to St Thomas

Aquinas it is a science that involves everything because everything reflects the creator.[14] Karl Rahner considers it to be 'a science of faith'.[15] The Jesuit theologian Gerald O'Collins explains that science here means 'an organised body of knowledge,' to which are applied 'critical methods of investigation and argument'.[16] If theology is a science with its own technical language and procedures, it might not appear to be readily accessible to anyone who is not trained in this discipline.

However, empirical theologians also recognise what has been called 'ordinary theology'.[17] This is the theology of the ordinary Christian. After all, theology comes from the Greek *theologia*, which incorporates two words *theos* meaning God and *logos* meaning 'word' or 'discourse'. It is essentially 'speaking of God'. One of the best known definitions of theology comes from St Anselm, who called it 'faith seeking understanding'.[18] Significantly this locates theology within a believing community. So theology involves believers speaking of God, a believing community giving expression to its faith.

It is this that empirical theologians, including those researching Catholic education, make use of when trying to understand the faith as it is lived out by believers. When we take part in liturgy or receive the Sacraments; when we speak out against injustice or campaign for a fairer world; when we reach out to the poor and marginalised, we are giving expression to our faith. We are speaking of God. We are doing 'ordinary theology'. When I interviewed headteachers as part of my research into their theological disposition, they did not use religious language. However, they did speak about the religious motivation behind their work and lives. This was a theological discourse. They were speaking about God. Through their work, their faith was seeking to understand more about what God intended.[19]

It has to be accepted that this 'ordinary theology' has deficiencies. It is often unsystematic and even confused. It is never-the-less a concrete expression of the lived faith of believers, who themselves are guided by the Holy Spirit. As such it is an important source of information about faith as it is experienced and lived. The respected Catholic theologian Richard McBrien recognises the pervasive presence of 'ordinary theology' when he says '...we are not even conscious of our faith except theologically. We cannot express it in words or in action, independently of theology'.[20]

For practical theologians and those researching Catholic education from a theological standpoint, 'ordinary theology' will be an important component of what has to be identified and reflected upon.

2. Embracing a Constructionist View of Reality

All research makes assumptions about the nature of reality and the foundations of knowledge, or to put it more technically ontological and epistemological assumptions. Unlike the early empiricists, modern exponents of empirical theology do not see social reality as existing independently of those taking part in it. They reject a 'positivist' approach that assumes that individuals can see, measure and describe the world as it really is. Instead they regard social reality as something that is constructed and interpreted by participants. The researcher is not regarded as an unencumbered observer but rather as an active participant, who interprets social reality through the lens of previous experience.

Drawing on Karl Popper's conclusion that social conditioning influences knowledge of whatever kind and Max Weber's contention that no research is value-free, van der Ven argues that all research takes place within a tradition with its own assumptions and value-judgements. The 'pure' and 'abstract' rationality, which liberal scholars regard as the currency of scientific research, is illusionary. Even the pursuit of 'objective facts' arises from a value judgement that acquiring these is worthwhile. Van der Ven considers it legitimate to use empirical methods to learn more about the experience and practice of those who embrace the tradition. He argues that in creating a research framework and drawing conclusions from the data collected, reference must be made to the theological tradition involved. In our case the Catholic Tradition which underpins Catholic education.[21]

Among the aspects of society that social science explores, theology is not alone in having its own traditions, theories and normativity. Social scientists researching education, culture, management and sport, for example, have to discover how those involved in these areas understand the enterprise in which they are engaged: the 'theories' that underpin their practice and how value is ascribed? According to van der Ven, anyone trying to extract meaning from the research data that they collect has to understand the tradition from which the data emanates.[22]

3. Valuing What the Researcher Brings

Van der Ven goes further and argues that it is only from within the tradition that empirical data about the tradition can be validly interpreted. Empirical research is concerned with the observation and interpretation of things as we experience them. This is never completely objective as the researcher brings a unique history with its own set of experience and way of seeing the world to the task. This is what Gadamer calls our 'situation' or 'horizon', which is all that we are capable of seeing from our particular vantage point.[23] Self-reflection may allow the researcher to be more aware of predispositions but van der Ven questions whether it is possible to compensate for them. In his view, we all come with assumptions and latent theories, which influence our interpretation of experience. Consequently all empirical research is 'theory-laden'.[24]

Gerald Grace is an eminent social scientist but surely when he takes the notion of 'social capital' and develops the concept of 'spiritual capital' he is drawing on his Catholic horizon.[25] When David Fincham discusses community with his MA students at St Mary's he quotes the social scientist Ferdinand Töennies, who distinguishes between community, which comes about through the choice of participants, and associations, which come about through necessity. This is a sociological distinction. However, Fincham then goes on to quote the Congregation for Catholic

Education, who speak of our schools as communities 'based on the call to witness to Jesus Christ and share his mission'.[26] Here he is drawing on his Catholic horizon. Many researchers into Catholic education will write about the 'sacramental perspective' in education or passing on the charism of a religious order to lay successors.[27] These draw on a Catholic horizon.

I like to imagine Gadamer's notion of horizon as a bubble, which we each inhabit individually. Not only does this bubble represent the extent of our capacity to see but is also represents the lens through which we see. Having been nurtured within the Catholic Church all my life I am sure that I see the world through a particular Catholic lens. It is beyond the scope of this essay to do more than indicate what this might include. As Catholics we know that all that God made was good. We recognise that we are indebted not self-sufficient, acknowledging that we are created by God, redeemed by Christ and destined to eternal life. We have a purpose to our life, an end point to which we are travelling. We know that people become fully human through communion with God and others. We have a sacramental imagination and consequently, through the eyes of faith (our horizon), we encounter God in all things. We encounter the holy in the mundane, the transcendent in the immanent and the divine in the human. These are some of the constituents of our Catholic horizon.[28]

There is the danger of a misunderstanding here regarding the 'active participation' of the researcher. My belief in God influences the way that I see the world. My view of the world influences how I attribute meaning and significance to what I experience.[29] However, the same is true of someone who does not believe in God. It is perhaps confusing to say that the researcher must not be biased as I am arguing that there is an implicit bias in everyone. What can be said is that the religious person as with any other researcher must try to understand different perspectives, must not simply seek evidence to support a pet theory, must report what is said accurately and not selectively (avoiding contrary evidence), must not assume that others (even other Catholics) share the researcher's understanding of religious concepts, be transparent in outlining methodology, process, evidence and interpretation so that others can judge the integrity of the research.

4. Being Theological Throughout

Empirical theologians ensure that their research is 'theological all the way through'.[30] The research question is expressed theologically. It may not be expressed in technical theological language but it must be intrinsically theological. As we have already seen the researcher needs to have an understanding of the tradition within which they are working. The language and practices of those who participate in the research has to be recognised as an expression of the lived tradition and as offering insights into their theological understanding.

Not all research into Catholic education can be described theologically. Research into the effectiveness of a new maths scheme may not be appropriately described in theological terms and would not fall within the scope of practical theology. However, when Morris claimed that performance against a number of criteria was better in Catholic schools that other similar institutions, he posited a Catholic effect.[31] Exploring that might well lead to a research question that can be expressed theologically.

In the earlier stages of its development empirical theology was a two stage process. Initially empirical methods were used to explore a particular situation and then theological reflection sought lessons for the faith community within that 'secular' data. This inter-disciplinary approach has now been superseded by an intra-disciplinary approach where the methods of social science are fully incorporated into a theological investigation where the language and concepts are theological.

I have to make it clear that I am not suggesting that there is a Christian or Catholic way of doing research. The methods that we adopt do not have to be religious in themselves. The methods used must produce empirically valid, reliable and publicly defensible results. What I am arguing for is the use of empirical methods to help us describe what we are researching from a theological point of view. I am also suggesting that this is what many researchers are doing when they research Catholic education.

5. Adopting a Circular Process

Care must be taken to make effective use of Scripture, systematic theology and, for Catholics, the teaching of the *Magisterium*, which has an authoritative status within the Church. Those researching Catholic education will pay particular attention to the Vatican II document[32] and documents emanating from the Congregation for Catholic Education or from Bishops' Conferences or Diocesan Bishops. They will also pay attention to theological reflections by academics. However, it is not a case of testing findings against Church teaching. It is a circular process, which allows personal experience to be enlightened by *magisterial* teaching, and *magisterial* teaching to be enriched by the experience of the faithful.

The process usually begins by gathering empirical evidence about the lived experience of participants. It is important to accept this as it is and understand it in its own context before trying to interpret it critically. What then follows might best be described as a 'conversation' between this critical interpretation and the contribution of theologians and the *Magisterium*. Church teaching is not allowed to predetermine the outcome of the enquiry, which as far as possible should be expressed in the language of the participants. This may lead to an interpretive theory or hypothesis, which may be tested empirically. The aim is to improve practice with which the process starts and ends.

The components of this process are:

1. the evidence from experience, which may be gathered empirically;

2. a critical interpretation of this within its own context;

3. the understanding of the Church, which will be gathered from the literature;

4. a conversation between the critical interpretation of experience and the teaching of the Church;

5. a new hypothesis to be tested empirically;

6. critical interpretation of the results of this enquiry;

7. formulation of proposals for future practice.

A Few Words of Caution

A degree of caution must be exercised when using concepts in our research that have meaning within the faith community. Often these concepts have been developed by academic theologians. We need to make sure that we understand the concepts. Sacramental perspective might be one example. *Koinonia*, Communion may be another. So I am not suggesting that we can play fast and loose with theological concepts. We must recognise what they mean but our research may extend or alter that understanding. In our research we will be able to draw on 'an organized body of knowledge' to quote O'Collins, and apply 'critical methods of investigation'.

Focusing on experience has other dangers. In particular, one must be careful that the divine is not reduced to the finite and definable, or that we are drawn to the conclusion that what we experience is all that there is. Not only is Revelation and Tradition diminished in this scenario but God can disappears from view altogether. To some extent we are able to protect ourselves from this error by reference to the *Magisterium* as a source of authentic Catholic teaching. This is not to reduce empirical theology to a means of determining whether Catholics hold 'correct' opinions but rather to have a firm point of reference which allows us to explore personal experience.

Conclusion

This chapter offers a theoretical perspective, which allows those researching Catholic education to adopt an empirical theological approach. It argues that 'ordinary theology' helps the researcher understand the lived experience of those involved in Catholic education. It assumes a constructionist view of reality, the value-laden nature of research and the benefits of research from within a tradition. It insists that the whole process is theological and that it adopts a circular process, which includes a critical interpretation of experience, a conversation between this critical interpretation and the tradition of the Church leading eventually to renewed practice and experience. Those interested in adopting this approach are recommended to read some of the key texts listed in the references.

Notes

1   Cf. R. R. Ganzevoort, 'Van der Ven's empirical/practical theology and the theological encyclopaedia'. In: C. A. M. Hermans & M. E. Moore (eds), *Hermeneutics and Empirical Research in Practical Theology, The Contribution of Empirical Theology by J. A. van der Ven* (Neatherlands: Brill, 2004). There are a number of ways of classifying theology. See P. A. Egan, *Philosophy and Catholic Theology: A Primer* (Minnesota; Liturgical Press, 2009), 25–31 and R. McBrien, *Catholicism* Third Edition (London: Geoffrey Chapman, 1994), 52, for examples. I have gone with Ganzevoort because I think that the various divisions included by others can all be incorporated within this model.

2   G. Baum, *Man Becoming: God in Secular Society* (New York: Crossroads, 1979), 9.

3   Vatican II, *Gaudium et spes* (1965).

4   K. Rahner, 'Practical Theology within the Totality of Theological Disciplines', *Theological Investigations* vol. IX, translated by G. Harrison (London: Darton, Longman and Todd, 1972), 101–114.

5   D. Tracey, 'The Foundations of Practical Theology'. In: D. Browning (ed.) *Practical Theology: The Emerging Field in Theology, Church, and World* (San Francisco: Harper and Row, 1983), 61–82.

6   Pope St John Paul II, Apostolic Constitution *Ex Corde Ecclesiae* (1990).

[7] For example, J. Sweeney, J. G. Simmonds, & D. Lonsdale (eds), *Keeping Faith in Practice: Aspects of Catholic Pastoral Theology* (London: SCM, 2010); K. A. Cahalan, 'Locating Practical Theology in Catholic Theological Discourse and Practice'. In: *International Journal of Practical Theology*, Vol. 15 (2011), 1–21; T. Beaudoin, 'Secular Catholicism and Practical Theology'. In: *International Journal of Practical Theology*, Vol. 15 (2011), 22–37; E. Foley, *'Siblings or 2nd Cousins-Once-Removed: A Relational Taxonomy for Practical Theology'*. In: *New Theological Review*, Vol. 26/No. 1 (September 2013).

[8] J. A. van der Ven, *Practical Theology: an empirical approach* (Kampen, The Netherlands: Kok Pharos, 1993), 111.

[9] W. K. Kay, 'Empirical Theology: a natural development?' *The Heythrop Journal*, Vol. 44, No. 2 (2003), 167–181; 177.

[10] Van der Ven, *Practical Theology*, 32.

[11] Cf. L. Green, *Let's Do Theology* (London & New York: Continuum, 2009). The origin on the pastoral cycle is generally attributed to the 'see, judge, act' approach developed by Joseph (later Cardinal) Cardijn, who developed the Young Christian Workers Movement early in the 20th century. It also has antecedents in the 'hermeneutic circle' of Uruguayan Jesuit theologian Juan Luis Segundo and Liberation Theology more generally. It is closely allied to the methodology of Catholic Social Teaching as illustrated in M. P. Hornsby-Smith, *An Introduction to Catholic Social Thought* (Cambridge: Cambridge University Press, 2006), 7 & 322. The influence of the pastoral cycle can be found in the other empirical theological approaches.

[12] Cf. H. Cameron, D. Bhatti, C. Duce, J. Sweeney, & C. Watkins, *Talking About God In Practice: Theological Action Research and Practical Theology* (London: SCM, 2010).

[13] Cf. van der Ven, *Practical Theology*; Kay 'Empirical Theology'; L. J. Francis, 'Personality Theory, Empirical Theology and Normativity'. In: J. A. van der Ven, & M. Sherer-Rath (eds), *Normativity and Empirical Research in Theology* (Leiden & Boston: Brill, 2004).

[14] St Thomas Aquinas, *Summa Theologiae*: Volume 1: Christian Theology translated by T. Gilby (Cambridge: Blackfriars, 1964 edition), 27.

[15] K. Rahner, 'Theology' in *Encyclopaedia of Theology: a concise Sacramentum Mundi* (London: Burns and Oats, 1975), 1687.

[16] G. O'Collins, *Foundations of Theology* (Chicago: Loyola University Press, 1966), 17.

[17] Cf. J. Astley, *Ordinary Theology: Looking, Listening, and Learning in Theology* (Burlington: Ashgate, 2002).

[18] St Anselm, *Proslogion*, translated by M. J. Charlesworth (London: Notre Dame Press, 1997 edition). St Anselm was an 11th century Archbishop of

Canterbury, theologian and doctor of the Church.

19 C. J. Richardson, *The Theological Disposition of Lay Catholic Headteachers: Evidence from two English dioceses* (Saarbrücken: LAP LAMBERT Academic, 2012).

20 McBrien, *Catholicism*, 40.

21 This argument is developed in J. A. van der Ven, 'An Empirical or Normative Approach to Practical-Theological Research'. In: van der Ven & Sherer-Rath (eds), *Normativity and Empirical Research in Theology*, 101–112.

22 *Ibid.*, 113.

23 H-G. Gadamer, *Truth and Method* (New York: Crossroads, 1985), 269 & 273.

24 Van der Ven, *Normativity and Empirical Research in Theology*, 106 & 109.

25 G. Grace, 'Renewing Spiritual Capital: an urgent priority for the future of Catholic education internationally'. In: *International Studies in Catholic Education*, Vol. 2/No. 2 (2010), 117–128.

26 Congregation for Catholic Education, *The Religious Dimension of Education in a Catholic School: Guidelines for Reflection and Renewal* (1988), 1.

27 Catholic teachers and leaders try to model themselves on Jesus Christ. They try to make Christ present for others. Their ministry has its origin in him. They become signs or sacraments of his ministry. This is what has been called the 'sacramental perspective'.

28 Amongst others T. Groome, 'What makes a School Catholic?' In: T. McLaughlin, *et al.*, (eds) *The Contemporary Catholic School: Context, Identity and Diversity* (Washington: Falmer, 1996), 107–125 has suggested distinctive features so has McBrien (1994) *Catholicism*, 8–15.

29 This argument is developed more fully in T. Cooling, *Doing God in Education* (London: Theos, 2010).

30 Cameron, *et al.*, *Talking about God*, 51.

31 A. B. Morris, *School Ethos and Academic Productivity: The Catholic Effect* (University of Warwick: Unpublished PhD thesis, 1996).

32 Vatican II, *Gravissimum Educationis* (1965).

PART II:
RELIGIOUS EDUCATION

4 RELIGIOUS EDUCATION REFORM IN THE CATHOLIC SCHOOLS OF ENGLAND AND WALES

Professor Anthony Towey and Philip Robinson

Anthony Towey is Director of the Aquinas Centre for Theological Literacy at St. Mary's University. He is the editor of 'The Pastoral Review' and a member of the Independent Commission on Religious Education convened by the RE Council of England and Wales.

Philip Robinson is a former head of an outstanding Religious Education department in St Aidan's Catholic School, Sunderland. He then served as a Religious Education Adviser to the Diocese of Hexham and Newcastle for four years. He is currently the adviser to the Catholic Education Service, the education agency of the Bishops Conference of England and Wales.

Blackadder and Jeremy Kyle

I T IS NO coincidence that the reform of key stage 4 and key stage 5 RE and indeed *all* public examination syllabi for 16–19 years olds in England and Wales was initiated while Michael Gove was education minister.[1] An historian by training, Gove was one of a number of scholars who had become increasingly frustrated at the narrow focus of secondary school studies of a past which seemed delimited by events of the Twentieth Century. Still worse, in a television age dominated by the need to entertain, the picture of those storied decades increasingly risked distortion. *Blackadder* was presented as a classic case, implying that the entire exercise of World War I was an exercise in utter futility.[2] Ignorant of the most fundamental military and diplomatic realities, school discussion of a subject as important as the Great War ran the risk of becoming an anachronistic discourse of emotional opinions rather than researched and reasoned argument.[3]

Meanwhile in Religious Education, a similar dilemma was emerging. Whilst RE was not included in the National Curriculum reform of 1988, it remained part of the Basic Curriculum and a statutory requirement for all schools.[4] Many RE Heads faced the problem that without any particular confessional tradition, their best option for keeping recalcitrant adolescents interested in classrooms was to go down the 'Big Questions' syllabus route. Besides classic religio/philosophical questions such as 'Does God exist?', even a Friday afternoon class could become animated by ethical debates on topics such as 'Sex before Marriage', 'Abortion and Euthanasia', 'Crime and Punishment', 'War and Peace'. Championed and resourced by luminaries such as Victor Watton and Peter Vardy[5], RE not only turned a corner in terms of examination entries, A-level Religious Studies mushroomed as teachers and pupils moved away from Scripture and Comparative Religions to follow pathways characterised by Philosophy of Religion and Ethics (PRE). One of the advantages of the approach was that everyone could join in classroom discussion without an assumed religious standpoint. The disadvantage was that without at least some religious standpoint, there was little to identify the discourse as essentially religious at all. At key stage 4 in particular, exam boards began to allocate marks purely for personal opinion and required no religious knowledge to answer certain questions.[6] The upshot was to leave many a puzzled academic wondering how A-level Theology had become Philosophy and many a puzzled diocesan inspector wondering when GCSE RE had become the Jeremy Kyle show.

The Trojan Horse

Whatever one might think of Michael Gove, the idea that subject disciplines should be recognisable by their distinct content and methodology is eminently reasonable. Moreover, since 'community cohesion' was part of the justification for maintaining the place of RE in the Basic Curriculum, there was further impetus to make sure that any reform of GCSE and A-level should emphasise religious dimensions of the discipline. In the round of consultations through 2014, Religious stakeholders were invited to participate in the framing of the new syllabi and in the first phase of exchange, there was a general sense that the reform would allow confessional traditions a great deal of control. All this changed with the 'Trojan Horse' crisis emerging from Birmingham in Summer 2014.[7] By now, Michael Gove had moved on and Nicky Morgan was faced with a claim that state-funded schools of non-confessional nature had become hotbeds of radical Islam. For the purposes of this article, whether this was by dint of governor neglect, complicity or deliberate forgery is neither here nor there; the politically sensitive nature of the problem directly led to Ms Morgan insisting that the RE reform should ensure that pupils would be exposed to the religious views and traditions of others. To that end, in a sudden directive, the DFE insisted that 25% of the syllabus at key stage 4 would have to be allocated to a second religion.[8] Not only did this rule out cosy comparisons between Christian denominations, it threw up the first of a number of challenges to teachers in terms of knowledge deficit. After all, it is one thing to ask pupils to draw a synagogue or draw a mosque. It is entirely another to elicit and answer questions on the theological sources of shema, tawid or brahma ... on a Friday afternoon.

CREDO

As a major stakeholder in the reform, the Catholic Church had some issues with this imposition. Accounting for 25% of all pupils taking GCSE and 20% of the A-level cohort, the custodians of the Catholic school system, the CES (Catholic Education Service) and NBRIA (National Board of Religious Inspectors and Advisers) joined forces with representatives from Catholic Higher Education institutions to discuss this and other matters relating to the reform. University concerns about standards in schools was one of the drivers for Gove's review since tertiary courses in various disciplines were finding even students with high grades ill prepared for the challenge of degree work in their respective subjects.

Under the umbrella acronym of 'CREDO' (Catholic Religious Education Development Opportunities), this group quite quickly came to a mind on a number of matters:

1. At KS4, whilst acknowledging there would be pedagogical challenges, the requirement to include more Catholic specific input was warmly welcomed.

2. At KS4, the pros of teaching of a second religion outweighed the cons. Mindful in particular of recent papal overtures towards Judaism, and aware of contemporary sensitivities regarding Islam, the initiative could be seen as advantageous in deepening religious reflection among pupils in Catholic schools.

3. At KS4, rather than studying the *beliefs* and *sources* of a second religion, *beliefs* and *practices* would be far more congenial and useful in terms of pedagogy and inclusivity.

4. The dominance of Philosophy and Ethics at A-level was not desirable in terms of transition to traditional theological courses at university.

5. In any review of the subject matter, there should be no privileging of the agnostic position which is discernible both in an uncritical comparative religions approach and in the design of numerous PRE specifications and assessments.

6. To nail the misconception that doctrine is desiccated catechesis, there should be a recognition that critical discourse occurs *within* not just across religious traditions.

7. Some refreshment of the philosophy of religion syllabi with more contemporary interlocutors was desirable.

It was gratifying for the group to see echoes of its discussions finding their way into eventual statutory Ofqual[9] documentation—particularly points 3–6. Moreover, under DFE headings of *sources, beliefs, practices* and *forms of expression*, the group was satisfactorily able to capture a spectrum of Catholic theological understanding in the regulatory 'annexe' by which examination boards were to design their specifications.[10]

A Fairly Civil War

When Ofqual released the first statutory recommendations, however, there was considerable consternation among teachers and Heads of RE. In retrospect this is hardly surprising. At KS5, the A-level proposal was radical, philosophy of religion and ethics were conflated and reduced to no more than half of the reformed A-level syllabus such that doctrinal and scriptural components could regain equal billing.[11] At KS4 while the government had made provision for several routes through the qualification, astute teachers could sense that if 50% was to be spent on Catholicism in Catholic schools and 25% on a second religion that would only leave 25% for 'themes' which would in turn force a choice for some between philosophy and ethics on the one hand or Mark's Gospel on the other. In dealing with the 100,000 pupils or so who find themselves in KS4 in Catholic schools, some teachers *may* have been doing *some* Catholic doctrine but certainly were not spending 50% of their time on it.[12] In short, busy teachers faced the prospect of redesigning courses on a huge scale looking for at least two years' worth of new material over KS4 and KS5.

These fears were compounded at A-level by a suspicion that a syllabus reworked in favour of doctrine and scripture would not be attractive to students. Students picking Religious Studies as their fourth 'AS' only to find it more stimulating than their core choices had meant year on year growth in the popularity of the subject at A2.[13] This not only altered perceptions regarding the academic credibility of RE in the school context, it had also helped breathe life into ailing theology and philosophy departments at Universities. All this was imperilled by the suggested KS5 reform which was strongly contested in terms of both rationale and scope by a number of schools as well as the aforementioned Peter Vardy and Victor Watton. The eventual compromise was that a 'three from four' model for A-level was adopted. Philosophy of Religion and Ethics were separated which meant schools could choose a syllabus which only required a one third modification in favour of doctrine or scripture whilst retaining two-thirds of their teaching allocated to Philosophy of Religion and Ethics.

Specifications

By now the development of specifications for the various examination boards was well under way. At KS4, the syllabi that emerged which addressed the preferred Catholic pathway were very different in their approach. It is fair to say that AQA engaged most closely with the CREDO group. Acting on their behalf, and using Catholic imagination as the watchword, our collaboration produced a thematic model beginning with forms of expression. Edexcel were more conservative in reproducing the pattern of their previous and very popular pre-reform specifications but touched base with CREDO regarding issues of theological clarity and density. Last, late but not least, the Welsh Board's English arm, Eduqas, approached us to help them adapt a pathway in their general specification which retained philosophical/ethical questions as a start point but followed the ramifications thereof into Catholic doctrine and practice. Since teachers had felt somewhat dictated to both by state and church, this did at least give some room to breathe and a sense of choice in terms of way if not what, in terms of method if not material.

At A-level though there was some direct contact with OCR, the response of the Exam Boards to CREDO was more detached. The market is much smaller, currently running at c. 25,000 for all entrants, perhaps 5,000 of whom are in Catholic sixth-forms. The very successful OCR syllabus saw relatively little change and along with Eduqas modelled patterns which included a discrete doctrinal component. While AQA adopted an approach which accessed philosophy and doctrine through ethical paradigms there was disquiet as it began to look as though none of the examination boards would offer any textual/ scriptural options.[14] Since this flew in the face of one of the aspirations of the KS5 reform in general and indeed of the CREDO group in particular, there was some anxiety before Edexcel saved the day by being the only board to interweave a textual/scriptural pathway into their specification.[15]

Reception of the Reform: Some Immediate Issues

Recalcitrance and Resourcing

It is fair to say that all teachers under the cosh of achievement indices and busy schedules need thoroughgoing reform like a hole in the head. For ourselves, attempting to familiarise practitioners with the salient elements of the reform has at times felt downright disloyal, downright presumptuous, downright rude and occasionally downright dangerous. Distinguishing between message and messenger has almost been a health and safety issue.

That said, beginning with national gatherings sponsored by the Catholic Universities (Liverpool Hope, Newman Birmingham, Leeds Trinity and St. Mary's Strawberry Hill), the CREDO group have undertaken to help resource the reform with and alongside the earnest, ongoing and more commercially driven response of publishers and educational enterprises. There are numerous text-books in the pipeline and new readers and web-resources along the way. Most gratifying of all is the common cause engendered by the reform which is leading to networks of resource sharing and best practice exchange.[16]

Second Religion

Once the shape of the reforms crystallised in early 2015, it was clear that for the average Catholic RE department, the teaching of the second religion was the most neuralgic concern. The problem was then somewhat simplified because the Bishops Conference further detailed that Judaism should be the religion chosen for fairly obvious theological if not sociological or political reasons. Whereas this caused a stir in the media with Catholic schools being accused of not teaching Islam (patently untrue, it is taught at KS3), one unintended effect may be the development of more concentrated expertise in Judaism at both diocesan and national levels.

In this endeavour, however, there needs to be caution. It may surprise some, but the 'comparative religions' approach associated with Ninian Smart is no longer considered methodologically sound. Directly echoing the views of the CREDO group, one of the reassurances that all the stakeholder religions received has been that the religion should be studied *in itself*. However, the tendency to *colonise* the religion of another by making its categories fit one's own is hard to eradicate and may be something that needs to be monitored, especially since the beliefs and teachings of Judaism are subliminally familiar to Catholic teachers through knowledge of the Hebrew scriptures.

Medium-term Issues

Attainment and Assessment

One of the most radical aspects of GCSE reform which affects all subjects is the new 1–9 grade structure. One view is that it offers more differentiation at the top end simply so that Russell Group universities can more easily identify the crème de la crème. From our experience, of more concern to the Catholic teacher is pitching the putative 'pass' mark at grade 5 which means that 66% of those currently receiving a grade C will *fail*. Since RE is currently one of the few subjects where Catholic schools often endeavour to enter everyone this will be an educational and emotional problem. RE is often taught by highly motivated teachers who somehow manage to get *that* pupil their one 'pass' at GCSE. This may well prove impossible now. The 'sweetener' for schools is that 'Progress 8' which measures improved performance rather than discrete attainment as the measure for success will replace '5 A-Cs' in the league table score-chart. Yet this is scant consolation on two fronts. As long as RE stays outside the EBac roster, it will continue to suffer the stigma that it is a second class subject. Still worse, it will not solve the more intimate issue of classroom motivation and domestic despair when a teacher, a pupil and a parent who have really tried, who have really tried, are told that they have 'failed'.

Raising the stakes on attainment means raising the stakes on assessment. It is worth emphasising that at every CREDO gathering of teachers the *first* thing practitioners want to see is the *last* thing they do—the *examination*. This teleological approach is actually acutely utilitarian since league tables, job security and pupil life chances force practitioners to *teach the exam*. Again, it is one of the fruits of the reform that some examination boards have had to review their SAMs (Sample Assessment Materials) to make tasks and expectations clearer such that marking might in turn be more consistent. Less clear, though, is how government, Church or school are going to spin the envisaged outcome of the reform which would see the quality of work improve against a background increased failure.

Meanwhile CREDO have voiced a concern regarding the recruitment and training of examiners for the reformed syllabi. At the moment, an experienced teacher after tax will rarely find an examination stint rewarding enough to justify the after-hours exhaustion. There are confidentiality problems which prevent school time being used for this work and the result is a significant amount of the work is done by NQTs and retirees who are not exactly representative of the practitioner base. It is to be hoped that more detailed and subtle aspects of the specifications will be vouchsafed by proper CPD so that assessment aberrations such as 'Catholics have a fundamentalist approach to Scripture' can be avoided otherwise the central aim of the reform will be undone.

Key Stage 3

The announcement of harder examinations for students at KS4 may have repercussions for praxis at KS3 (11–14 year olds). The temptation to retroject curriculum activities into Year 9 is understandable and some might say desirable. By chance or providence, however, a project reviewing the KS3 curriculum for Catholic schools is already in train and has not yet been set in stone.[17] Without instrumentalising everything in the service of public examinations, those reviewing the KS3 materials may well have an important role to play in laying the groundwork for the more demanding redesign of KS4.

Long-Term Issues

No Religion

Ever since the first consultations on the reform, there has been a cacophonous if not quite orchestrated response from the BHA (British Humanist Association). Counter intuitively, they are founder members of the Religious Education Commission (REC) and do not wish to see RE removed from the curriculum but rather express a desire to see atheism taught as a 'religion'. Despite the inherent incoherence of such a position, the voices of humanism have ululated long and loud and show no sign of abating. They are currently agitating for a review of the provision which in classic Whitehall fashion has been somewhat dead batted.[18] It is perplexing and distracting that much of the rhetoric voiced is impressionistic and anecdotal, but since their evident aim is elimination of state support for faith schools, their lobby must be taken seriously.

Scripture and Sources

At KS4 it is unclear as to how many Catholic schools will choose thematic pathways through the Bible as opposed to pathways in philosophy and ethics. It may be as few as one in ten and is not

→ can they be meaningful co-inspected?

even an option on the approved Eduqas route B. In fairness to
the working of the reform, Gove's historian instincts do mean
that the importance of sources including scripture is emphasised
at all times and in almost all argumentation. In turn this *may*
mean that more mature understandings of certain key texts such
as Genesis will emerge.

At KS5, the reluctance to offer textual pathways was in part
educational since the statutory requirements still require a
'synoptic/synthetic' question connecting the different strands of
the A-level. It is simply much more straightforward for specification designers to identify links between ethics-philosophy and
doctrine than between any combination involving text. That said,
for some of the examination boards it was a more pragmatic
decision not to allocate resources to the design and moderation
of such pathways give recent pitiful uptakes of biblical options.

While for HEIs this has killed off one of the hopes they had
for the reform that future students might arrive at universities
schooled in the rudiments of textual analysis, writ large, it has
wider implications. The accelerating diminution of biblical
literacy over the past decades may in the first instance be a
Christian/Catholic/confessional issue but it may yet prove to have
cultural ramifications way beyond the educational purview as the
21st Century unfolds.

Teacher Training and Transmission

Prescinding from the ideological tensions of whether school
based or university based ITT is best for equipping teachers for
classroom success, there is no doubt that the reform will require
a different portfolio of expertise for trainees. It is fair to say that
subject knowledge in the recent past has not emphasised core
doctrinal components in a way that could have been presumed
until the 1990s. Many able practitioners of RE in Catholic schools
are more confident of teaching lessons on meta-ethics and Kant's
Categorical Imperative than lessons on the Incarnation.

Linked to this are wider concerns regarding theological transmission and the core purpose of Catholic schools. While it is wrong to place all the burden of mission and ethos of schools on RE departments, there is no doubt that if teachers trained in theology are unable to articulate the wonder and defend the reasoning of the Catholic tradition, the future will be bleak.

Concluding Remarks: RE Reform and the Future of Catholic Schools

Though triggered by mainly pedagogical concerns on the part of government, the authors believe that the GCSE and A-level reform of RE will prove to be a pivotal moment for Catholic education. RE is central to the purpose and existence not just of our secondary schools but is also foundational to our primary provision and indeed to our HEIs. Despite the thoroughgoing challenge of the reform, it has led to unprecedented levels of co-operation between policy makers, advisers, practitioners and academics through the CREDO group. This in turn has led to unprecedented levels of engagement with examination boards in the design and assessment structures of their RE specifications. Given the welcome variety of examination options at GCSE, it may well be that concerted work at KS3 will turn out to be equally important for the inculcation of a Catholic methodology across our provision, but no longer should there be any opposition between theological integrity and examination success at KS4.

The 'community cohesion' aspect of the reform is both understandable and appreciated in the current context. In numerous meetings, Catholic teachers have affirmed an aspect of the discipline which is not necessarily shared by other subjects on the curriculum, viz., 'RE must be a safe place to discuss difference.' The *dialogical* nature of the pedagogy in RE need not be lost in the Reform and indeed should be encouraged wherever possible.[19]

Building upon these positives, ecclesial and educational custodians of our religious heritage must be continue to cooperate in order to equip teachers and pupils with the doctrinal dexterity necessary to articulate anew the Catholic tradition for the 21st century. That this should be critical, constructive and respectful of conscience goes without saying. That the reform should be properly rooted in Scripture, Tradition and Magisterium is likewise desirable. At stake is the transmission of Catholic wisdom and in this sense the reform quite properly has more resonance with apologetics than catechesis. Happily, recent events such as the Synod and the Family and the encyclical *Laudato Si'* amply demonstrate the living conversation that seasons Catholic wisdom with the signs of the times. If our classrooms can capture the sense of this dynamic tradition, the heroic challenge of the moral life, the beauty and imagination of Christian belief and expression, then another generation may yet be inspired to give their lives to the cause of Catholic education.

Notes

[1]   Gov.uk Website: Oral Statement to Parliament by Michael Gove, The Education Secretary on Education Reform, 11 June 2013: See: https://www.gov.uk/government/speeches/oral-statement-on-education-reform.

[2]   R. Curtis & B. Elton, *Blackadder 4: Blackadder Goes Forth* (London: BBC, 1989).

[3]   See for example Gordon Corrigan's *Mud, Blood and Poppycock* (London: Cassell, 2004) which in challenging the 'lions led by donkeys' narrative manages to be at once researched, reactionary, popular and polemical.

[4]   Education Reform Act 1988, Section 2 (UK government legislation). See: http://www.legislation.gov.uk/ukpga/1988/40/section/2/enacted. RE has never been part of the National Curriculum (NC) since the NC applies to all schools and faith schools were exempt from state control of RE. Also, parents retained the right to withdraw from RE whilst they had no such right to withdraw from the NC. As such, RE was considered part of the Basic Curriculum but not the National Curriculum – statutorily required but without its content being prescribed by the state.

[5]   See for example V. Watton, *Religion and Life*, 5th edn (London: Hodder, 2013). Likewise, P. Vardy & P. Grosch, *The Puzzle of Ethics* (London: HarperCollins, 1999).

6   Thus while 'Discuss the Divorce Law in the UK' might appear in a 2015 RE paper, it might be more properly addressed in Sociology or Law or Politics.

7   P. Clarke, Report into allegations concerning Birmingham schools arising from the 'Trojan Horse' letter. Return to an Address of the Honourable the House of Commons (22 July 2014). See: https://www.gov.uk/government/uploads/system/uploads/attachment_data/file/340526/HC_576_accessible_-.pdf

8   Department of Education (UK), Reformed GCSE and A Level subject content consultation: content consultation (launched 7 December 2014). See:https://www.gov.uk/government/uploads/system/uploads/attachment_data/file/372136/Reformed_GCSE_and_A_level_subject_content_consultation.pdf

9   Office of Qualifications and Examinations Regulation (Ofqual).

10 Department for Education, Religious Studies: GCSE subject content (February, 2015). See: https://www.gov.uk/government/uploads/system/uploads/attachment_data/file/403357/GCSE_RS_final_120215.pdf

11 At this stage, sixth forms had to pick 'two from three' options, viz. Philosophy and Ethics; Text; Study of a Religion.

12 This foreboding was confirmed by a directive from Bishop Malcolm McMahon on behalf of the CBCEW (Catholic Bishops' Conference of England and Wales) in August 2015.

13 A-level RS has hitherto enjoyed a steady upward trend and has tripled in entrant numbers since the 1990s. The total number of RS A Level candidates in June 2015 was 25,773, within spitting distance of economics and well ahead of political studies and ICT/computing. See: 'Student Performance Analysis – National Percentage Figures for A Level Grades': http://www.bstubbs.co.uk/a-lev.htm

14 Symptomatically, in early drafts of AQA A-Level Christianity, the specification did not even mention Jesus.

15 Even here, however, PRE retains its hegemony since it is impossible to combine Doctrine with Scripture.

16 Perhaps of especial note is Catholic REsource, a website curated by Andy Lewis, M.A., who also helps co-ordinate the London RE Hub and is now based at St Bonaventure's, Forest Gate, London.

17 'People of God: Called to Serve' is the working title of the project.

18 The BHA (British Humanist Association) launched a Judicial Review in which they claimed it was claimed that aspects of the GCSE reform were contrary to human rights law. This was partially upheld. See: https://www.judiciary.gov.uk/wp-content/uploads/2015/11/r-fox-v-ssfe.pdf. The DfE (Department for Education) considered appealing the

judgement but instead published guidance which effectively dismissed the claims of the BHA and sidestepped the judgment. See: https://www.gov.uk /government/uploads/system/uploads/attachment_data/file/488477/RS_ guidance.pdf. This has not gone down well with the BHA (see https://humanism.org.uk/2015/12/29/44457/) and we understand the BHA is currently considering whether it will take legal action over the guidance note.

[19] As an example of good practice, the CREDO designed AQA (Assessment and Qualifications Alliance) specification actually enshrines dialogue as a method when discussing ethical themes.

- "the sickness of long thinking"
  Chippewa Proverb

- ⤷ how does this relate to "yugen" –
  the "profound awareness of the
  universe that triggers feelings too
  deep and mysterious for words"?
  (Japanese)

5 THE SICKNESS OF LONG THINKING: RELIGIOUS EDUCATION AND THE NEW JUNIOR CYCLE

Dr Amalee Meehan

Amalee Meehan PhD, is Associate Professor of Religious Education with Dublin City University. Her recent publications include 'The Message of Mercy' (Dublin: Veritas, 2015), 'Joining the Dots: A Programme of Spiritual Reflection and Renewal for Educators' (Dublin: Veritas, 2012), and three Religious Education textbooks for US Catholic high schools as part of the Credo Series.

Introduction

IN STEF PENNEY'S award winning novel *The Tenderness of Wolves*, the trapper Parker tells Mrs Ross of an abandoned wolf cub he once found and brought up as a dog. That is, until:

> It remembered it was a wolf, not a pet. It stared into the distance. Then one day it was gone. The Chippewa have a word for it—it means 'the sickness of long thinking'. You cannot tame a wild animal, because it will always remember where it is from, and yearn to go back.[1]

There is something at the heart of every living thing that remembers where it is from and yearns to go back. At some unfathomable depth there is a pull, a tug, reminding us of who we really are. It is an insight as old as the Scriptures, true for instance of the Prodigal Son. Luke tells us that when the younger son has hit rock bottom, alone in a foreign land and tending pigs, he 'comes to himself' (Lk 15:17). He recognises something about his own identity and place in the world. In that dawning realisation the younger son understands who he really is, where he is from, and yearns to go back.

In this article I will set out how the sickness of long thinking is a phenomenon today, typified by the increasing loneliness documented among young people, and by an ongoing spiritual hunger prevalent in Western culture. Identity and rootedness, or more accurately, lack of both—both personal and communal—is at the heart of this sickness; only by addressing who and whose we are can healing take place. This is where religious education— here specifically Christian religious education—has a clear and vital function. Identity and rootedness, and discovering who and whose we are, lie at the heart of religious education. First disciple Andrew's encounter with Jesus presents a paradigm of this. It demonstrates how Christian religious education in its fullest sense can have a transforming effect. In the concluding section I will show how Christian religious education can contribute significantly to the vision and values of the new Junior Cycle in Irish second level schools,[2] and towards healing the sickness of long thinking.

Loneliness and Isolation

Our postmodern culture is characterised by a rootlessness showing itself in a diminished sense of the past, a kind of cultural amnesia, a lostness and loneliness. With no sense of who we are or where we came from, a new isolation takes hold.

For instance, in 2010 the UK Mental Health Foundation found loneliness to be a greater concern among young people than the elderly.[3] The 18 to 34 year olds surveyed were more likely to feel lonely, to worry about feeling alone and to feel depressed because of loneliness than the over-55s. Linked to depression, paranoia, anxiety, addiction, cognitive decline and a known factor in suicide, loneliness can be both a cause and effect of mental health problems.

Dr Grant Blank, a survey research fellow at the Oxford Internet Institute, points out that social media and the internet can be a boon and a problem.[4] They are beneficial when they enable us to communicate with distant loved ones, but not when they needlessly replace face-to-face contact. People often present an idealised version of themselves and their social lives online. Comparing friends' seemingly perfect lives with ours can lead us to withdraw emotionally and socially. Indeed, a 2013 study of social media at the University of Michigan found that Facebook reduces life satisfaction.[5]

For Ruth Sutherland, the chief executive of Relate, the antidote to reducing our isolation rests on laying the foundations to good-quality relationships earlier in life. But good quality interpersonal relationships depend on self-awareness, integrity, compassion and empathy—the ability to walk in the shoes of the other.[6] Healthy relationships depend on these qualities—exactly the qualities that characterise the life, death and resurrection of Jesus of Nazareth.

Spiritual Hunger

The human instinct to ask questions and the quest for meaning is nothing new. This is reflected in core parts of the Irish Junior Certificate Religious Education syllabus. Introduced in 1990, the Junior Certificate is a state programme in the Republic of Ireland resulting in a terminal examination. Students take the Junior Certificate examination after three years of second level education, at age 15 approximately. Religious Education (RE) can be taken as a Junior Certificate examination subject, on an optional basis. The RE syllabus, while appropriate for all students whether they have a particular religious commitment or not, seeks to go beyond information giving to contribute to the spiritual and moral development of the students. For this reason, many schools that do not offer RE as an examination subject still follow the syllabus with their Junior Certificate students.

The opening section of the Junior Certificate RE syllabus focuses on historic and contemporary expressions of the search for meaning. But our traditional modes of searching have been fractured. Instead of guiding us down the road of long thinking, contemporary quests tend to lead us around in circles. The fallout is an acute spiritual hunger tied to a sense of desolation. Nowhere is this clearer than in the burgeoning shelf space given over to new age spirituality and self-help manuals in the all the major book stores.

Let's take for example, Oprah's Book Club. When the show concluded in May 2011, Nielsen Book Scan created a list of the top-10 bestsellers from the Club's final 10 years (prior data was unavailable). The top three bestsellers are as follows:

- Eckhart Tolle, *A New Earth: Awakening to Your Life's Purpose* (2005), 3,370,000 copies
- James Frey, *A Million Little Pieces* (2003), 2,695,500 copies
- Elie Wiesel, *Night* (1960), 2,021,000 copies

It is interesting that in different ways, all of these books point to the acute spiritual hunger referred to above. Take for instance, the most popular choice: *New York Times* multi best seller Tolle's *A New Earth*. According to Tolle, the book's purpose 'is not to add new information or beliefs to your mind or to try to convince you of anything, but to bring about a shift in consciousness'.[7] He envisions a world population that is increasingly more humble, enlightened and pure and that involves a massive change in group think. When Eckhart Tolle, partnered Oprah for a series of webinars based on the book, they attracted more than 11 million viewers.

Pope Francis is acutely in tune with this spiritual hunger: 'The great danger in today's world, pervaded as it is by consumerism, is the desolation and anguish born of a complacent yet covetous heart, the feverish pursuit of frivolous pleasures, and a blunted conscience'.[8] For Francis, the joy of the Gospel, the rootedness of the Kingdom as preached and lived by Jesus, is a sure way to consolation, contentment and real fulfilment. Herein lies the basis of a compelling argument for religious education as a core element of the new Junior Cycle. This is a theme I will return to.

Identity and Integration

By turning us towards who and what we are and always have been, Christian religious education has much to offer the sickness of long thinking. At its core is the fundamental claim that 'the joy of the Gospel fills the hearts and lives of all who encounter Jesus.'

Jesus begins his ministry by proclaiming the good news that the Kingdom of God is now at hand for all who are ready to receive it (Mk 1:14–20). There is something so compelling about both messenger and message that many who hear it leave their old lives and become disciples.

Andrew is a typical example. Like many of the first disciples and many of us, Andrew is a searcher. When we first meet him in John's Gospel, he is a disciple of John the Baptist—a young man looking for something more to life. But he is not sure what that 'something' might be. Andrew sees Jesus walking by and senses that in this man he will find what he is looking for. Jesus takes the initiative and welcomes him into his company; he invites him to 'Come and see'. Then he asks one of the most fundamental questions of life: 'What are you looking for?' (Jn 1:35–42). What is the aim or purpose to your life; what are you looking for inside yourself, what are you looking for in me, Jesus? It is the question he still asks of us today. His offer set us free from inner emptiness and loneliness is constant.

Through this prolonged encounter Andrew realises that he has found something essential to his identity, integrity and to where he belongs. His sense of himself is transformed and his first response is to bring his brother to share the experience. 'He first found his brother Simon and ... brought [him] to Jesus' (Jn 1:41–42). It is noticeable that the transformation of Andrew is both personal and communal. We hear very little of Andrew for the remainder of the Gospels, but when we do, he is invariable bringing people to Jesus. That extraordinary 'coming to himself' which happens to him through his encounter with Jesus propels him again and again to share it with others.

Knowing the person of Jesus and his message of the Kingdom of God continues to have a transforming effect on generations of people, just as it did on the first disciples. The word 'Kingdom' does not refer to a place, but to the power of God which is rooted in love. Wherever the love of God prevails in our world, the Kingdom is there. It suggests a matrix of interdependent loving relationships with self, others, God and the created world—very different to the loneliness and confusion previously described.

Christian Religious Education

It is important to say from the outset that Christian education is committed to academic excellence. This is achieved through respecting the different disciplines while challenging students to achieve their potential across the curriculum. A successful education is one which provides students with the ability to draw from the rich treasures of both faith and reason in order to contribute towards a future that holds promise for all.

Christian religious education then is a subset of Christian education. It has particular significance because like all religious education, it deals with ultimate questions. How we answer those questions cannot but influence our values, view of life, and the choices we make. Our identity is inseparable from our faith—whether religious or not. It is not something we park at the school gate and take up again as we leave the schoolyard.

At its core, Christian religious education formally and informally, helps students into a warm and loving relationship with God. The ultimate aim is to help bring about the Kingdom of God, that God's will for 'fullness of life for all' may be 'done on earth as it is in heaven'.[9] God's Kingdom was Jesus' sense of purpose; this is the meta-criterion that guides what and how we teach.

In other words, Christian religious education informs, forms, and transforms people's lives, enabling them, by God's grace, to become disciples to Jesus as 'the way, the truth, and the life' (Jn 14:6) and 'for the life of the world' (Jn 6:51). At its best, Christian religious education reaches people at the level of heart and hands as well as head. In other words, rather than an exclusively academic exercise, it is a deeply holistic and relational knowing that helps people to know and manage themselves, and relate positively and constructively to the world around them.

While remaining true to the faith of the (Catholic Christian) community, Christian education also turns us out toward an intercultural, inter-religious society. This is increasingly important in a society that takes pluralism seriously. There is an expanding discourse of inclusion and respect for otherness while recognising the distinctive challenges and identity of our faith tradition.

Jesus himself reminded 'in my Father's house there are many dwelling places' (Jn 14:3). The challenge for religious educators is to ground people in the particular while opening them to the universal. For Christians, every articulation of the story and vision must turn us toward the neighbour in love, including the neighbour who is 'other' rather than 'the same'.

Religious Education and the New Junior Cycle

The National Council for Curriculum and Assessment (NCCA) has taken an integrated approach towards the new Junior Cycle, which will replace the Junior Certificate programme. Traditionally, learning was centred on a series of independent subjects with their own aims and course objectives. The *Framework for Junior Cycle* (2011) is based on a set of principles, 24 statements of learning and eight key skills. According to the NCCA, it is underpinned by research evidence, public and political consensus, professional concern and many years of consultation.

The *Framework*

> describes what all junior cycle students should learn. It provides national qualifications associated with learning in junior cycle. But it also gives school management and teachers the professional space and flexibility to decide how best to organise the learning and adjust it to meet the learning of their students.[10]

Only three subjects are compulsory for Junior Cycle qualification—English, Irish and Mathematics. Other subjects such as

Religious Education may or may not be included in the programme offered by a particular school, as long as the school meets
the requirements of the *Framework*.

Key skills at the centre of the new Junior Cycle include
managing myself, staying well, communicating, being creative,
working with others and managing information and thinking.
Depending on how a school designs its curriculum to meet these
key skills among other requirements, time devoted to subjects
such as religious education may be substantially decreased. In
other words, the role of religious education in second level
education is by no means guaranteed with these reforms.

However, the new Junior Cycle expects that through education
the person will be ready, willing and able to make a contribution
in the world at large. The values 'fundamental to the vision' are
equality and inclusion, justice and fairness, freedom and democracy and respect for human dignity and identity. There is a clear
resonance between these values and those which characterise the
Kingdom of God as preached by Jesus.

We have already seen how Christian religious education is a
deeply holistic and relational. Indeed, its aim is at one with that
of the new Junior Cycle—to help people to know and manage
themselves, and relate positively and constructively to the world
around them. With its emphasis on identity and integration,
Christian religious education has much to offer not only to the
teaching and learning emphasis of the new Junior Cycle but to
the loneliness and spiritual hunger described earlier.

Conclusion

The human search for completeness is as prevalent as ever and
resonates through popular culture. Christian religious education
has much to offer in this context. In keeping with the vision of
the new Junior Cycle it places the person at the centre, emphasising the importance of personal integration, good relationships
and participating positively with community and society. In fact,

because the Christian tradition shares much of the vision and values of the new Junior Cycle, it is well placed to contribute to many of the principles and key skills outlined in the framework document. Parents who wish to have their teenage children educated in their faith tradition can know that this tradition fully compliments the new Junior Cycle. But they must insist that religious education is not dropped a central component. The best chance of realising the vision and values of the new Junior Cycle depends on sufficient emphasis given to religious education.

Notes

[1] M. Clarke, Euro Crime Review of S. Penney's, *The Tenderness of Wolves* (London: Quercus, 2007) April 2007. See: http://www.eurocrime.co.uk/reviews/The_Tenderness_of_Wolves.html (accessed 3 May 2015).

[2] The Junior Cycle in Irish second level schools is a three year cycle for students aged approximately 12–15. Although the emphasis of this article is on the role of Christian Religious Education in the new Junior Cycle, it has resonance with any holistic approach to education, particularly one rooted in the Christian faith tradition.

[3] J. Griffin, 'The Lonely Society?' (London: Mental Health Foundation, 2010) See full report: http://www.mentalhealth.org.uk/content/assets/PDF/publications/the_lonely_society_report.pdf (accessed 10 April 2015).

[4] G. Black, cited in N. Gil, 'Loneliness: A Silent Plague that is Hurting Young People Most' *The Guardian,* 20 July 2014.

[5] E. Kross, P. Verduyn, E.Demiralp, J. Park, D.S. Lee and N. Lin *et al.,* 'Facebook Use Predicts Declines in Subjective Well-Being in Young Adults', *PLoS ONE,* Vol. 8, No. 8: e69841 (14 August 2013) http://journals.plos.org/plosone/article?id=10.1371/journal.pone.0069841 (accessed 10 April 2015).

[6] R. Sutherland, cited in N. Gil, 2014. Relate is a UK relationship counselling organisation. See www.relate.org.uk.

[7] R. Tolle, *A New Earth: Awakening to Your Life's Purpose* (London: Penguin Group, 2005), 6–7.

[8] Pope Francis, *Evangelii Gaudium* (2013), 2

[9] T. H. Groome, *Sharing Faith: A Comprehensive Approach to Religious Education and Pastoral Ministry* (Eugene, OR: Wipf & Stock, 1991).

[10] National Council for Curriculum and Assessment (NCCA), Towards a Framework for New Junior Cycle (Dublin: NCCA, 2011), 13.

6 APPROACHING THE CATHOLIC RELIGIOUS EDUCATION CURRICULUM IN SCHOOLS

Dr Anne Hession

Anne Hession is an Assistant Professor of Religious Education and Spirituality, in the School of Human Development, Dublin City University. She is the author of Catholic Primary Religious Education in a Pluralist Environment (Dublin: Veritas, 2015).

EDUCATION, WHEREVER IT is carried out, is always based in some kind of worldview, religious or secular. In the Catholic school, the process of education is mediated through a Christian as opposed to a secular world-view. Thus, while other approaches to religious education (phenomenological, sociological, historical, conceptual, and ethnographic) might invite students to examine religion from a secular philosophical position, the Catholic religious education curriculum will approach religion from a Catholic insider's theological point of view.[1] Catholic teachers are heirs to a rich tradition of thought on education, a tradition which is continually appropriated and transformed by them, in light of the differing historical and socio-cultural contexts in which Catholic education is carried out. The recently published Catholic religious education curriculum for pre-school and primary in Ireland, provides an interesting exemplar of the dialogue between theology and education in Catholic religious education; of the need for sensitive inculturation of Catholic educational principles and practices in the context of the broader state-mandated curriculum in Catholic schools; and of the way in which Catholic educational theory impacts upon concrete religious education practices at primary level.[2]

Catholic Religious Education: Two Dimensions

Catholic religious education involves two inter-related dimensions: formation or nurture for healthy commitment in Christian faith and critical education which fosters students' critical understanding of their own religious faith as well as openness to others, valuing their insights beliefs and experience.[3] The *formative* dimension of Catholic religious education describes the process whereby the student is invited to acquire some of the knowledge, ways of knowing, feelings, attitudes, values, skills, behaviours and sensibilities that being Christian involves. This formation should provide a balance of the cognitive, affective and behavioural dimensions of knowing in Christian faith.[4] The *critical* dimension of religious education involves critical understanding of and debate about religion, both one's own and that of others. A critical approach to one's own religious tradition protects students' freedom of conscience, aiding the development of an autonomy-enhancing, critical and authentic faith.[5] At all times, Catholic religious education aims to promote the dialogue between faith and reason, enabling students to relate their spiritual, moral and religious lives to their developing intellect and to the culture in which they live. In this way, the religious education curriculum supports the development of a form of Catholic religious identity that could be characterised as 'committed openness', or 'openness with roots'. Ultimately, religiously educated Catholics will be persons who understand, appreciate and live their own faith, while being capable of entering into real dialogue with people whose life commitments are different from their own.

A Unique Aim

Catholic religious education understands religious faith as a trusting relationship with Jesus Christ. Christian faith involves apprehending the world and our place in it in a particular way and living a distinctive way of life in company with others. Therefore, the goal of Christian religious education is to enable children to immerse themselves in Christian religious beliefs, practices and values, inviting them to live inside the Christian vision of the good life. Recent Catholic teaching on education distinguishes the tasks of religious education and catechesis.[6] One important consequence of this distinction, is that 'Religious Instruction (sic)' in schools must adopt a scholastic shape, presenting the Christian message and the Christian event with 'the same seriousness and the same depth with which other disciplines present their knowledge'.[7] This means that religious education is similar to other subjects on the curriculum in that it provides a systematic, age-appropriate and orderly initiation into a particular intellectual tradition or body of thought.

At the same time, religious education can be distinguished from other subjects in the curriculum. On this point, the Congregation for Catholic Education declares that the 'fundamental difference between religious and other forms of education is that its aim is not simply intellectual assent to religious truths but also a total commitment of one's whole being to the Person of Christ'.[8] As a result, the formal religious education curriculum is understood as making an indispensable contribution to the holistic formation of the human person offered by Catholic schools, especially in the area of faith formation.[9] This means that the goals of Catholic religious education are very different to the goals of other subjects that comprise the curriculum. The challenge is to translate these goals into educational theory and methods that express the uniquely Catholic approach to religious education in schools.

Education and Theology in Dialogue

Catholic religious education is interdisciplinary in nature, drawing on the disciplines of theology and education for its underlying principles, theories and values.[10] The relationship between theology and education in Catholic religious education is one of creative tension. On the one hand, the understanding that God works in and through the conditions of creation requires that religious education be based on the best contemporary understanding educators have of the learner and of the way the learner learns. For this, religious educators will draw on the social sciences and on contemporary philosophy and educational theory in general.[11] Teachers need to be clear that their understanding of child development, their instructional methods, their teaching strategies and their methods of assessment enable them to achieve their stated goals. In this way, contemporary educational theory and experience will inform Catholic religious education's framing of the Catholic faith Tradition, leading to a creative re-interpretation and inculturation of the religious tradition for the differing societal and cultural situations in which religious education is being carried out.

On the other hand, Catholic theology informs religious educational practice such that Catholic educators will always be careful to incorporate the methods and insights of the social sciences, philosophy and general education into an overall theological perspective.[12] This means that contemporary psychological, philosophical and sociological perspectives on human development will be brought into dialogue with the images of the person and of personal development proposed by Catholic theology. While not denying the validity and applicability of the images of the person underpinning the social sciences, Catholic theology proposes an image of the person which has greater explanatory power over a wider range of experience than do those proposed by the social scientist.[13] The crucial addition offered by Catholic anthropology is the person's openness to Transcendence. Further, in distinction from the view of the learner as an individual autonomous self, the learner in the Catholic school will be viewed as one who is in a relationship with God, as one who is a subject of Revelation and as one who is part of a faith community. In sum, the models of the human proposed by the social sciences or contemporary educational models in any context will be examined carefully in light of the images of the human offered by Catholic theology.

Designing the Religious Education Curriculum

Catholic religious educators tend to work in a state system of education that has its own standards, procedures and curriculum models. Hence, what Sullivan has termed 'the double allegiance— to religious fidelity and to professional standards—of those who work in such schools'.[14] Catholic curriculum writers must engage with these models and standards, not least because teachers are professionally trained to engage in lesson planning in particular ways in differing societies, but also because teachers need to be able to integrate their planning of the religious education curriculum with other subject areas. It would be a mistake, however, for Catholic teachers to adopt the outcomes-based philosophy and pedagogical strategies of other subject areas in an uncritical fashion, thus assuming religious education to be the same as other subject areas of a Catholic schools' curriculum.[15] For example, teachers will be particularly wary of the logic of instrumental reasoning, imported into education. Instrumental reasoning is that form of reasoning that acknowledges only one goal that is, effectiveness—it is good if it works. Educational strategies that are too tightly tied to the extrinsic utilitarian goal of effectiveness, too tightly tied to the methodology of cost-benefit analysis will not be capable of reflecting the unique approach to religion offered by Catholic schools.

Approach to Religion

There is a world of difference between approaching religion as revealed or as something constructed. In a constructivist approach to religion, religious beliefs and values are understood as human constructs which are subject to multiple interpretations. Religious beliefs or truth claims, in this view, are internal to the language game being played. In a constructivist approach to religious education, therefore, the whole idea of a search for ultimate truth will be rejected or at the very least, side-lined. In contrast, Catholics approach religion as having its origins in a divine Truth revealed by God. The educational activity of the Church addresses the faith of hearers who, through God's grace, freely accept the good news of God's salvation by a personal faith response. Therefore, in Catholic religious education, religious beliefs possess an epistemic status and normative quality that is denied to beliefs understood merely as cultural constructions.[16] Further, because Christian faith invites a free response, it demands a pedagogy that enables people to hear God's truth received in revelation, to understand and judge it for themselves and to commit to the concrete living of Christian faith in the world.[17] This unique approach to religion is reflected both in the way in which learning outcomes are crafted and in the pedagogical approaches used in the Catholic religious education curriculum.

The Catholic Preschool and Primary Religious Education Curriculum for Ireland

Religious education is one of seven areas on the Primary School Curriculum in both the Republic of Ireland and in Northern Ireland.[18] The Irish Episcopal Conference provides the curriculum framework for Catholic religious education of young children in both jurisdictions.[19] This national curriculum provides an interesting example of how Catholic religious education has been given a unique configuration to respond to the particular socio-cultural context of Irish primary schools.[20] The final section of this chapter will explore some of the ways in which this curriculum honours the principles of Catholic religious education discussed above.

We note, first of all, that the *educational* rationale which underpins this religious education curriculum is expressed in its aim. The curriculum seeks 'to help children mature in relation to their spiritual, moral and religious lives, through their encounter with, exploration and celebration of the Catholic faith'.[21] This aim conveys the understanding that Catholic religious education is an academic discipline which offers children a systematic and rigorous education in Christian faith in order that it might assist in and promote their spiritual, moral and religious development. Relating the aim of religious education to the process of the pupils' own spiritual, moral and religious maturation gives the curriculum a clear educational focus by saying what exactly religious education in the Catholic school contributes to the personal development of the child. Further, the aim respects the distinction between catechesis and religious education thus honouring the fact that children in Catholic schools will have different capacities to engage with the gospel of Jesus Christ. The curriculum requires teachers to take those differing capacities seriously and to ask what there is in the Christian Tradition that might contribute to the spiritual, moral and religious development of *all* children engaged in religious education in the Catholic school.

Second, we note that the curriculum prescribes a set of religious education outcomes *and* a set of faith formation goals for four, six, eight, ten and twelve year olds. This means, first of all, that the outcomes-based paradigm has been accepted as a standard way in which curricular materials are presented in the Irish educational context and as a useful way of helping teachers to understand the content, methodologies and processes integral to Catholic religious education. The provision of *religious education outcomes* for each age-level offers teachers a clear focus for their work; provides a clear sequence of progression in religious learning across the primary school; assists teachers in integrating religious education with other subject areas of the curriculum; and allows for the assessment and evaluation of student achievement in a way which is helpful for future planning.[22] At the same time, the provision of *faith formation goals* in the curriculum serves to remind teachers that the ultimate horizon for religious education in Catholic schools is the development of lived Christian faith in discipleship of Jesus. The *faith formation goals* are an important complement to the *religious education outcomes* in the curriculum, not least because teachers' hopes or goals in the area of faith development cannot be assessed, as it is inappropriate to formally assess personal or spiritual change in students.

Finally, we note that the metaphor of 'religious literacy' is used in the curriculum to describe an approach to educational outcomes that reflects the unique character of religious education in the Irish Catholic school.[23] Here the metaphor of 'religious literacy' empowers teachers to adapt (and therefore also to subvert) the outcomes based paradigm which teachers use in other areas of the curriculum. By outlining what it means to be a *religiously literate* six, eight, 10 or 12 year old, the curriculum outlines the ways in which young children are invited to engage with the Christian Tradition and the skills and processes distinctive of learning in the Catholic religion at primary level. Skills of religious literacy are grouped under five categories: understanding, communicating, participating, developing spiritual literacy and developing inter-religious literacy.[24] The application of a religious-literacy framework to the curriculum enables teachers to re-interpret the outcomes paradigm according to a humanistic vision, thus giving expression to the formative and critical dimensions of religious education in the Catholic school.[25]

Religiously Literate Catholics

To conclude, the desired outcome of Catholic religious education is spiritually mature young persons who have a life-giving relationship with Jesus Christ, with their own 'inner selves', with others and with the whole of creation; who have the knowledge and skills—appropriate to their age and capacity—to think and communicate spiritually, ethically and religiously; who are discovering the meaning and significance of their lives as children; who are developing a sacramental imagination, capable of recognising the presence and salvific action of God in their lives; who are learning how to engage creatively and critically with their religious tradition; who are becoming aware of the strengths and limitations of the culture in which they live; who have the confidence that they are loved and a developing ability to cope with religious and moral failure; who are developing a capacity for worship and a sense of belonging to a religious community; and, finally, who are learning that personal religious faith is linked to the work of justice, civic responsibilities, and empathy and solidarity with all.

Notes

[1] P. R. Hobson & J. S. Edwards, *Religious Education in a Pluralist Society: the key philosophical issues* (London: Routledge Falmer: Woburn Press, 1999), 22.

[2] Irish Episcopal Conference, *Catholic Preschool and Primary Religious Education Curriculum for Ireland* (Dublin: Veritas, 2015).

[3] For a detailed exploration of the categories of formation and critical education applied to Catholic religious education see A. Hession, *Catholic Primary Religious Education in a Pluralist Environment* (Dublin: Veritas, 2015), Ch. 5.

[4] T. H. Groome outlines the three dimensions of knowing in Christian faith in *Christian Religious Education: sharing our story and vision* (San Francisco: Harper & Row, 1980), 56–63. Pope Francis refers to three educational languages: 'the language of the head, the language of the heart, the language of the hands' in Pope Francis, Address of the Holy Father Francis to the World Congress Organised by the Congregation for Catholic Education (21 November 2015).

[5] On faith-based education that enhances autonomy, see T. H. McLoughlin, 'Parental rights and the religious upbringing of children'. In: *Journal of Philosophy of Education*, Vol.18/No. 1 (1984), 75–83. For the Church's stance on religious freedom See Vatican II, *Dignitatis Humanae* - Declaration on Religious Freedom (1965); Congregation for Catholic Education, *The Religious Dimension of Education in a Catholic School* (1988), 6. See also Congregation for Catholic Education, *Lay Catholics in Schools: Witnesses to Faith*, (1982), 42.

[6] Congregation for Catholic Education, *The Religious Dimension* (1988), 68; Congregation for the Clergy, *General Directory for Catechesis* (1997), 73; Congregation for Catholic Education, *Circular Letter to Presidents of Bishops' Conferences on Religious Education in Schools* (2009), 17.

[7] Congregation for the Clergy, *General Directory* (1997), 73.

[8] Congregation for Catholic Education, *The Catholic School* (1977), 50.

[9] *Ibid.*, 50–51; Congregation for Catholic Education, *The Religious Dimen-*

sion, 69.

[10] The Magisterium of the Catholic Church has yet to offer a document which offers a rationale for the conceptual framework, aims, purposes and methodologies of *school-based* religious education. In the absence of such a document, contemporary religious educators tend to draw on principles of catechesis, contemporary theological resources, as well as on the social sciences for the formation of Catholic educational theories. See: L. Franchi, 'Catechesis and Religious Education: a Case Study from Scotland'. In: *Religious Education: The official journal of the Religious Education Association*, Vol. 108/No. 5 (2013), 467–481.

[11] Congregation for Catholic Education, *The Catholic School*, 52.

[12] D. Heywood, 'Theology or Social Science? The Theoretical Basis for Christian Education'. In: J. Astley & D. Day (eds), *The Contours of Christian Education* (Great Wakering, Essex: McCrimmons, 1992), 113.

[13] D. Heywood, *Theology or Social Science?* (1992), 99–116. On the way in which the language of social science excludes the Transcendent from educational discourse see A. Thatcher, 'Policing the Sublime': a wholly (holy?) ironic approach to the spiritual development of children'. In: J. Astley & L. J. Francis (eds), *Christian Theology and Religious Education* (London: SPCK, 1996), 117–139.

[14] J. Sullivan, 'Faith Schools: a culture within a culture in a changing world'. In: M. de Souza et al., (eds), *International Handbook of the Religious, Moral and Spiritual Dimensions in Education*, Vol. 1 (Dortrecht: Springer, 2006), 938.

[15] B. Hyde, 'A Category Mistake: Why Contemporary Australian Religious Education in Catholic Schools may be Doomed to Failure'. In: *Journal of Beliefs & Values*, Vol. 34/No. 1 (2013), 36–45.

[16] L. P. Barnes, *Education, Religion and Diversity* (London, New York: Routledge, 2014), 204.

[17] On the necessity of provision for the act of judgement in Catholic religious education, see R. Topley, 'The Act of Judgement in Religious Education: Light from Newman, Lonergan, Giussani and Groome'. In: P. Kieran & A. Hession (eds), *Exploring Religious Education: Catholic Religious Education in an Intercultural Europe* (Dublin: Veritas, 2008), 234–248.

[18] Religious Education takes place in primary schools in the island of Ireland within circumstances supported by Education Acts in both jurisdictions. For the Republic, see Government of Ireland, Education Act (Dublin: the Stationery Office, 1998); for Northern Ireland see the Education Reform Act (1988) and the Education Reform Order (1989).

[19] Irish Episcopal Conference, *Catholic Preschool and Primary Religious Education Curriculum for Ireland* (Dublin: Veritas, 2015).

20   The Magisterium of the Catholic Church has yet to offer an authoritative document which offers a rationale for the conceptual framework, aims, purposes and methodologies of *school-based* Catholic religious education. In the absence of such a document, local Catholic Churches and their associated educational agencies enjoy the relative freedom to configure religious education syllabi and curricula that fit their own socio-cultural context. See Franchi (2013), 'Catechesis and Religious Education'.

21   Irish Episcopal Conference, *Catholic Preschool and Primary Religious Education Curriculum* (2015), 31.

22   The curriculum provides a 22-page appendix (163–185) which outlines cross-curricular links and opportunities for integrated studies with the Primary School Curriculum in the Republic of Ireland: Department of Education and Science, Primary School Curriculum (Dublin: The Stationery Office, 1999).

23   The term 'religious literacy' in the Irish context denotes an approach to religious education which is strongly catechetical in inspiration. In other contexts 'religious literacy' has come to be seen as a metaphor for an approach to religious education that is strictly educational as distinct from catechetical. See: B. Dwyer, 'Religious Literacy: a useful concept?' In: M. Ryan, (ed.) *Echo and Silence: Contemporary issues for Australian Religious Education* (Wentworth Falls: Social Science Press, 2001), 117–125.

24   Skills for understanding are rooted in children's capacity for attentiveness, intelligence, reasonableness and responsibility following the epistemology outlined by B. Lonergan. For a detailed explanation of these categories, see Hession (2015), *Catholic Primary Religious Education*, Chapter 6.

25   On the importance of interpreting the skill paradigm according to a humanistic vision and on the need to eschew a merely functional view of education which reduces education to skills about knowing and knowing how to do, see Congregation for Catholic Education, 'Educating Today and Tomorrow; a renewing passion', *Instrumentum laboris* (2014), 12.

7 RELIGIOUS EDUCATION IN CATHOLIC SCHOOLS: CONTEMPORARY CHALLENGES

Dr Sean Whittle

Dr Sean Whittle is a Visiting Research Fellow at Heythrop College, University of London, and at St Mary's University in Twickenham. He is also a Research Associate with the CRDCE, with Professor Gerald Grace. Alongside these academic roles he works part-time as a secondary school RE teacher at Gumley House FCJ Catholic School in West London. In recent years he has been collaborating with other academics working in the field of Catholic education in order to create the 'Network for Researchers in Catholic Education'.

Introduction

THERE IS LITTLE doubt that in Catholic schools in England and Wales Religious Education continues to enjoy a central role and highly favoured status. Indeed the sheer amount of curriculum time that is devoted to Religious Education is one of the most obvious distinguishing characteristics of a Catholic school in the UK. It is not uncommon to hear Religious Education described as the 'core of the curriculum'[1] in the Catholic school. Many of these schools give pride of place to Religious Education within their prospectus and promotional material. In these documents, it is often listed as the primary subject, coming before English, Mathematics and science. This stands in marked contrast to the status of Religious Education in most schools outside the Catholic sector, including some other types of faith schools. In many respects, Catholic schools are like fruitful oases for Religious Education, where the subject is valued, protected and indeed often celebrated as the central part of the school's *raison d'etre*. However, there is increasing evidence that the desert is beginning to encroach on these oases, and that even in Catholic schools, there are significant contemporary challenges facing Religious Education. This chapter will briefly identify what these challenges involve and how they are starting to threaten these fruitful sites for Religious Education. Before launching into this it will be necessary to draw attention to what is often seen as the largely positive state of the subject within the contemporary Catholic school in England and Wales.

The Healthy State of Religious Education?

On many levels Religious Education in Catholic schools has been basking in a sustained golden time over the past three decades. Paradoxically the upheaval generated by the implementation of the 1988 *Education Reform Act* which ushered in the National Curriculum, the GCSE examinations, school league tables and OFSTED actually had some positive effects for Religious Education in Catholic schools. Although the introduction of these 'market forces' within state education has been heavily criticised,[2] there have been some largely unintended (and on the whole) positive consequences for Religious Education in Catholic schools. Prior to the introduction of the GCSE examination not all pupils took public exams in *Religious Studies* in Catholic schools, but from 1990 onward it became normal for all pupils to take it. As a result, Religious Education Departments continued to expand and the status of the subject began to be enhanced. As headteachers began to grapple with the intricacies of league table positions, pupil attainment in Religious Education began to matter much more because it could also feed into the school's overall status. From those early years of the Religious Studies GCSE examination teachers in Catholic schools became increasingly adept at helping pupils to gain good results. No doubt the hefty chunks of curriculum time dedicated to Religious Education in Catholic primary schools, as well as at Key Stage Three (lower secondary) played a significant role in fuelling the levels of attainment in these public examinations. At the same time the development of exam specifications marketed specifically for Catholic schools blended in many of the topical debates, from 'abortion' to 'euthanasia' that older pupils found more engaging. The development of these 'Catholic' papers was facilitated by the introduction of the curriculum directory for religious education or RECD.[3] This document, first published in 1996 (and then substantially revised in 2012), serves as the 'National Curriculum' subject guidance for Religious Education in Catholic schools. In contrast to the situation facing Religious Education in all other schools, which drew their guidance from the local SACRE,[4] this meant that the subject content was nationally determined and linked with the modern magisterium by being couched in terms of the four primary documents promulgated during Vatican II. The underpinning provided by this RECD helped to further enhance the status of Religious Education in Catholic schools during the 1990s.

A further benefit of the RECD is that it played a role in helping with the emergence of a benign inspection framework for Catholic schools. Both the Anglican and Roman Catholic bishops had been successful in lobbying for a separate inspection as part of the OFSTED system from when it was first introduced. This allowed for inspectors appointed by the bishops to inspect on their behalf both the Religious Education and religious ethos of the school. In terms of what the inspectors are looking for one of the hallmarks of effective Religious Education departments in secondary schools or Religious Education Co-ordinators in primary school is to ensure that content, teaching and learning is fully compliant with the RECD. Since the inception of these 'Section 48' inspections Catholic schools have become increasingly better at meeting the approval of the inspectors. On diocesan websites, there is abundant evidence of Catholic schools having good or outstanding provision for Religious Education.[5] The presence of a separate inspection system has helped to further enhance the status of the Religious Education department within the Catholic school. In practical terms, it means that every five years the spotlight is shone directly on this department and achieving the accolade of being designated as 'Good' or 'Outstanding' in terms of Religious Education and Catholic ethos has become important priority for the headteacher and the Governors of Catholic schools. The net effect is that over the past three decades the role of Head of Religious Education or being the Religious Education Co-ordinator in a primary school has become an important one in a Catholic school. It is not uncommon for these post holders to be automatically part of the Senior Leadership team. There is anecdotal evidence that a large proportion of the Leadership teams in Catholic schools teach Religious Education. All this means that in the average Catholic school Religious Education is regarded as the flagship department, with all pupils taking a GCSE in Religious Studies, with up to ten percent of curriculum time being allocated for the subject. It is hard to overstate the marked difference with the status of Religious Education in other types of school.[6]

Alongside the 1988 *Education Reform Act* another education policy that had a remarkably positive impact on Religious Education in Catholic schools were the reforms to sixth form studies known as '*Curriculum 2000*'.[7] The advent of this, which overhauled A- Levels, introducing a system where students first sat four AS Levels at age seventeen, before going on to take three onto A-Level at age eighteen, resulted in a very large expansion of the numbers electing to study Religious Studies in the sixth form. It shifted from being a minority subject to being a more mainline option for students. This surge in uptake was closely linked with the development of courses in which students could focus on two popular subjects: the philosophy of religion and ethics. This helped to fuel a sense in which Religious Education is very much on a par with the other core subjects: with all students being compelled to take the GCSE and large numbers of students electing to take up the subject in the sixth form. Within a relatively short span of years Religious Education in Catholic schools took on a more academic feel as it became increasingly focused on preparing pupils and students for public examinations. In order to compensate for this movement away from more general Religious Education there has been the development of lay-chaplaincy within Catholic schools over the last two decades. The chaplain will run retreat days, prepare liturgies and be a person who is available to offer spiritual support to both pupils and staff. In large part this is because the rest of the Religious Education team are too busy preparing pupils for the examinations. This too has fuelled the contemporary perception that in Catholic schools Religious Education is first and foremost an academic subject.

Not only does Religious Education in Catholic schools receive a significant amount of curriculum time each week but there are also many layers of support for it both locally and at national level. Almost all of the Catholic diocese in England and Wales employ advisors who support Religious Education in Catholic schools, both primary and secondary. As a result, classroom teachers have access to support from key specialists in Religious Education. In a time of public sector austerity and the demise of Local Authority provision (in the wake of schools opting for Academy status) having this level of support for Religious Education in Catholic schools is impressive. These advisors collaborate with the inspectors appointed by the Catholic bishops, forming a *National Board of Religious Education Inspectors and Advisors* (NBRIA) who meet regularly to support the provision and quality of Religious Education in Catholic schools in England and Wales. A further layer of support is provided through the *Catholic Education Service,* in terms of political lobbying and ensuring that the interests of Religious Education at Catholic schools are represented at a national level. Religious Education in Catholic schools does not face the perpetual challenges and threats that the subject faces in so many non-Catholic schools.

During this golden time—spanning nearly three decades— Catholic schools have become fertile oases for Religious Education. In so many respects Religious Education in Catholic schools is well regarded and judged to be successful. Advocates of Catholic education are quick to point out that evidence from inspection reports is very positive.[8] Inspectors regularly designate high proportions of the Religious Education provision in Catholic schools as good or outstanding. Research indicates that pupils have positive attitudes to RE[9] and that there is ample evidence from school league tables that achievement in terms of public examinations in Religious Studies GCSE and A-Level is high for Catholic schools. In most Catholic schools a hefty slice of available curriculum time is given over to teaching Religious Education. The majority of Religious Education teachers are well qualified and on the whole, there are just about enough of them to go around. The oasis metaphor can be pushed a little to suggest that in recent years the sands of the desert are beginning to encroach and perhaps the signs are that this golden time has begun to slip away. In what follows a number of contemporary challenges to Religious Education in Catholic schools will be identified. It will be argued that many of these are rooted in the profound changes in education policy initiated after 2010.

Challenges Facing Religious Education in Catholic Schools

Just as the golden period described above was triggered, largely unintentionally, from education policy initiatives the more recent encroachment of Religious Education in Catholic schools has been caused by a number of subtle but significant shifts in educational policy which have trickled into effect since 2010 onwards. The most obvious of these are reforms to public examinations, both the GCSE and at A-Level, which were initiated whilst Michael Gove was Secretary of State for Education. The reforms implemented back in 2000 with the introduction of AS and A-Levels was reversed and all A-Levels returned to being two year linear courses with terminal examinations. It marked a return to the majority of students taking three subjects throughout their time in the sixth form. Similarly, GCSEs were to be restored back to being two year courses, with terminal exams. Given the dominance of public examinations for Religious Education in Catholic schools these changes by themselves would have been more than challenging enough. There was however a further complication in that the changes to the Religious Studies specifications became embroiled in concerns about radicalisation and the Government initiatives aimed at 'preventing' this from happening. In many respects, this was largely a result of the so called 'Trojan Horse' affair. Under the guise of a faith-based education, five Muslim schools in Birmingham were suspected to have been infiltrated by hardliners and were accused of allowing the radicalisation of Muslim pupils. Part of the government response to this involved further modifications to the Religious Studies specifications that were being reviewed. It became a policy that these specifications could not allow a school to focus on just one religion such as Islam, Buddhism or Catholic Christianity, to be studied in detail. Pupils at GCSE and students at A-Level had to study two different religions. It was hoped that learning about more than one religion would help pupils to engage positively with religious diversity and help to foster social cohesion. Moreover, there was a suspicion that in some schools pupils were learning just about the dominant religion found in that particular school or locality. In September 2016 the revised Religious Studies GCSE and A-Level specifications were implemented across all schools in England and Wales.[10] For the GCSE examination, it has resulted in seventy-five percent of time being devoted to one religion, with the second religion having the remainder of time. For Catholic schools this has been a significant change because it is no longer be possible for pupils to take a GCSE which is exclusively about Catholic Christianity. At A-Level, the dominance of the popular philosophy of religion and ethics options was significantly reduced through the introduction of a third paper drawn from key themes in one of the world religions.

It is important to spell out why these changes to the Religious Studies examinations amount to major set challenges for Catholic schools. The issues at stake are not simply practical ones about the difficulties of implementing new courses and increasing workloads and pressures on both teachers and pupils. These practical challenges do of course need to be properly acknowledge, not least because in Catholic secondary schools these public examinations dominate the entire Religious Education curriculum. It is not uncommon for pupils to be set work at Key Stage Three Religious Education which deliberately reflects the style of the GCSE exam questions that is taken at age sixteen. This is justified in terms of being a helpful preparation for the pupils. The hope is that after four or five years of answering GCSE exam style responses the pupils will be highly proficient when it finally comes to the real thing. Changes to the public examinations in Religious Studies will inevitably have trickle-down effect on the teaching and learning in Religious Education in earlier years in Catholic schools. Beyond these practical challenges there are other more substantive issues. One of these surrounds the choice of which 'second' religion ought to be studied as part of the GCSE course. Rather than this being a matter for each school to decide for itself, perhaps based on local geographical considerations or the skills and professional judgements of the teachers, it was taken as a more fundamental question. This is because decisions about the content of Religious Education are linked with the relationship between the local Catholic bishop and the schools within his diocese who are recognised as Catholic. In terms of ecclesiastical law (the Code of Canon Law) the local bishop is able to determine the Catholic character of a school within his diocese.[11] Part of his prerogatives is controlling the content of the Religious Education curriculum, and in England and Wales this is stipulated through the RECD. However, when the Government reforms imposed the study of a second religion in the public examinations they brought about changes to the Religious Education curriculum in Catholic schools. Both practically and symbolically it was Government policy that was determining part of this curriculum rather than the local Catholic bishop or his representatives. This is an issue of power and control. It amounts to a significant challenge about who ought to decide what the content of RE should be in Catholic schools in England and Wales.

In response to this Government policy the decision over what the second religion should be taught was decided centrally by the Bishops and the *Catholic Education Service*. Their decision is that Judaism must be the second religion studied alongside Catholic Christianity in all Catholic schools for the GCSE in Religious Studies. The choice of Judaism as the second religion is in many respects deeply puzzling, not least because in the UK this is one of the smaller religions present in society and it ignores the demographic indicators which suggest that Islam would be the more obvious choice.[12] A case can be made for arguing that the English and Welsh bishops and the *Catholic Education Service* chose Judaism in a deliberate ploy to mitigate the impact of having to study a second religion as part of the GCSE course.[13] Perhaps the basis for this attempt to mitigate the Government policy is an unacknowledged conflation between the study of the Bible with contemporary Judaism. As such it might well be that what initially looks like a clever way of avoiding the force of the policy might in the nitty-gritty of the RS GCSE lesson prove to be an overly complex and illusive relationship to teach. Again, the real challenges are not the practical difficulties faced by Religious Education teachers in Catholic schools but that in the struggle to control the content of Religious Education it is Government policy rather than Bishops who proved successful. This challenge is about who should be able to determine the content of Religious Education in Catholic schools. In an attempt to rebalance the arrangements, the RECD is currently being revised in order to accommodate the requirement to study a second religion. The RECD had already been revised in 2012 and further revision had not originally been scheduled.

The changes at A-Level have not proved as controversial, partly because there was no centralised imposition from the bishops about which religious tradition had to be studied alongside the philosophy of religion and ethics components. However, the real concern are fears over the possibility of declining numbers taking Religious Studies A-Level. As the reversal of the Curriculum 2000 reforms take full effect more Catholic sixth forms require students to take three rather than four subjects. This reduction in student choice looks set to erode the take up level of Religious Studies in the sixth form. There is a real possibility that it will slip back to being a more specialist or minority A-Level subject. This is a subtle but tangible diminution of the academic status of Religious Education in Catholic schools.

A further diminution of this status has come through the introduction of the 'English Baccalaureate', known more colloquially as the E-Bacc. When the Conservative Education Secretary, Michael Gove, introduced plans for an *English Baccalaureate* in 2011, he chose to exclude Religious Studies GCSE as an eligible subject. Naturally all RE teachers found this disappointing, but amongst advocates of Catholic education in England and Wales there was a particularly strong outcry. The CES made statements against it[14] drawing attention to the widespread concern that this downgraded the status of Religious Education even in Catholic schools. If GCSE Religious Studies is not eligible to be one of the qualifying examinations for the *English Baccalaureate* there is a concern that in system of school league tables headteachers might no longer see Religious Education in the same positive terms. This policy decision signals a changed context which means for some Catholic schools it is much harder to justify devoting ten percent curriculum time to Religious Education. The status of the subject, even in Catholic schools is now integrally bound up with the importance attached to the GCSE. Paradoxically there is a sense in which that golden period in which Religious Education in Catholic schools started to perceive itself primarily in academic terms is now proving to be a problem for the subject. In the light of the E-Bacc and concerns over declining sixth form numbers there is an emerging sense that the academic status of Religious Education is being questioned.

Is it Time to Recognise Afresh the Catechetical Element of Religious Education?

One response to the changing perceptions about the status of Religious Education in Catholic schools is to reconsider its relationship with catechesis. Examination courses can be effective ways of assessing knowledge of factual information or the ability to evaluate issues in the light of Catholic beliefs. However, they do not lend themselves to assessing faith formation. This means as pupils prepare for their GCSE there is an inevitable drift away from catechesis. This stands in stark contrast to the more overt catechetical focus of Religious Education in Catholic primary schools. Within the primary school there is a much closer link between classroom Religious Education and the preparation for sacraments and involvement in the local parish. This catechetical focus resonates much more closely with official Church teaching on Catholic education.[15] These documents explain that the primary role of Catholic education in general, and Religious Education in particular, is to assist parents in the task of bringing up their children within the Catholic faith.

This links with the wider theological and philosophical question about what Catholic schools are for? Are Catholic schools primarily confessional, in that their fundamental goal is to nurture pupils in the Catholic faith? Or is there a more general account of Catholic education which is distinct from nurturing the Catholic faith of pupils? The way these questions are answered has a profound effect on what the purpose of Religious Education is taken to be. On the one hand, if Catholic education is confessional then a key challenge for Religious Education is to respond to criticisms about its failure to produce young people who continue to practice their faith after they have left school.

There is a widespread perception that young people, despite being educated for thirteen years at a Catholic school, do not practice their faith in their adult life. This can be described in terms of 'bricolage'[16] where pupils pick and choose the elements of Catholic faith they prefer and jettison other aspects, such as regularly practising their faith. Another facet of this argument has been developed which points to the failure of Catholic schools, and Religious Education in particular, to yield young people who practice their faith.[17] This amounts to a fundamental problem for the future development or survival of the Catholic Church. In important respects, Religious Education is failing to achieve one of its primary goals. The answer lies in refocusing it along catechetical lines. As such ensuring pupils practice their faith, rather than gaining examination success in Religious Studies GCSE, ought to be the most fundamental priority for Religious Education in Catholic schools. On the other hand, if Catholic education is not characterised in these confessional terms, then Religious Education is faced with the challenge of clarifying what its primary purpose ought to be. Is it merely one of the subjects that typically make up the curriculum? Guidance documents issued by the Vatican[18] assert that that Religious Education plays a foundational role in the whole curriculum. However, justifying this claim is a tricky business, especially if Religious Education is not being characterised along catechetical grounds. Any attempt to make one particular subject, whether it be English, mathematics, science or even Religious Education, the core curriculum is fraught with difficulties. The supporting arguments typically trail off into assertions and slogans about the aims of education. At the heart of debates within the philosophy of education is the difficulty of deciding which of the competing aims of education ought to be pursued. These debates about the aims of education are ongoing and this makes for a challenging situation for Religious Education in Catholic schools. The nature of this part of the curriculum is bound-up with the ongoing questions about what the primary aims of a Catholic education ought to be.[19]

The Changing Composition of Catholic Schools

An emerging contemporary challenge for Religious Education in Catholic schools is to do with the increasing levels of religious diversity amongst the students who belong to Catholic schools. There has always been a wide diversity of beliefs represented in Catholic schools, not least because of the range of differing beliefs that are part-and-parcel of the Catholic Christian world view. However, in recent decades there has been an increasing trend amongst Catholic Christians to educate their children outside the Catholic school system. The annual census data from the Catholic Education indicates that significant numbers of non-Catholics are being educated in English and Welsh Catholic schools.[20] The contemporary reality in England and Wales is that most Catholic schools are not the preserve of Catholics alone. The presence of pupils who are 'strangers to the faith'[21] has in many respects tended to be largely ignored in the Religious Education curriculum in Catholic schools. An important challenge facing Religious Education in Catholic schools is to address this issue. These schools have a responsibility to both Catholic and non-Catholic pupils to foster religious literacy across more than just Catholic Christianity. The increasing levels of religious diversity in Catholic schools, which look set to continue, is something that the Religious Education curriculum needs to be far better at engaging with. This is because Catholic schools are not immune from the wider problems that beset Religious Education in all schools. Some research has been conducted which helpfully describes how all schools, including Catholic ones, struggle to teach religious literacy.[22]

At the more general sociological and political level the place of religion in society is being reassessed. The unfolding political events since 9/11 and the rise of *ISIS* or the so called 'Islamic State' demonstrate that religion is often not some private affair that is largely benign. Moreover, the long-heralded decline of religion and victory of secularism has not actually happened. Increasing numbers of sociologists are moving away from the secularisation thesis. Rather than being a waning feature of human existence, interest and concern with religion has increased since the year 2000. Naturally attention is on education and what ought to be the place of Religious Education within all schools. The role of religion in education and of Religious Education has become an important issue for education policy makers and there might well be further instances of the Government dictating what needs to be taught in Religious Education in Catholic schools.

Concluding Comments

There are other contemporary challenges to Religious Education in Catholic schools that could be raised, in particular concerns over the future supply of suitable teachers. However, the final observation is to lament the lack of leading and authoritative voices who champion the cause of Religious Education in English and Welsh Catholic schools. Whilst there are numerous skilled teachers, accomplished teacher educators and leading practitioners advising and inspecting Religious Education in Catholic schools there is a conspicuous lack of eminent voices researching and guiding the subject in England and Wales. Even the briefest survey indicates that the situation is very different in other countries. In Ireland the leading authority is Dr Gareth Byrne, associate professor of Religious Education at Dublin City University. In Scotland Professor Stephen McKinney heads a team which has heavy research interests in Religious Education and catechesis. Religious Education in Catholic schools in the USA have an able champion in Professor Thomas Groome. Whilst Canada has both Professor Graham McDonough and Professor Richard Rymarz (originally from Australia). Yet in England and Wales there is no similar leading voice driving the subject forward and engaging with the challenges the subject now faces. Perhaps the biggest challenge facing Religious Education in Catholic schools in England and Wales is to find way of nurturing some champions who will navigate a path through the more challenging times for Religious Education in Catholic schools that lie ahead over the next two decades.

Notes

[1]   For example see the summary statement on Religious Education on the Catholic Education Service website (see www.catholiceducation.org.uk › Lesson Resources › Religious Education).

[2]   See: G. Grace, *Catholic Schools: Mission, Markets and Morality* (London: Routledge Falmer, 2002).

[3]   Catholic Bishops' Conference of England and Wales, *Religious Education Curriculum Directory of Catholic Schools and Colleges in England and Wales* (London: Catholic Education Service, 2012).

[4]   The Religious Education curriculum in state schools is determined locally through a representative body known as the Standing Advisory Council on Religious Education (SACRE).

[5]   For example see the Westminster website education which has copies of all Section 48 Inspections carried out in recent years: http://www.rcdow.org.uk /education.

[6]   For a fuller discussion of this, see S. Whittle *Researching Catholic Education: Contemporary Perspectives* (Singapore: Springer, 2018).

[7]   These reforms were first introduced in September 2000.

[8]   For example see A. Morris, *Fifty Years On: the case for Catholic schools* (Essex: Matthew James Publishing Ltd, 2008).

[9]   See: P. Manghan, *Re-Imagining the Catholic Secondary School in Wales in the Twenty-First Century: the voice of the students* (unpublished PhD thesis, Bangor University, 2015). This research into Catholic schools in Wales identified many positive student responses about RE in Catholic schools. Although A. Casson (2012) is critical of Catholic education, this study does include some largely positive student responses in *Fragmented Catholicity and Social Cohesion: faith schools in a plural society* (Oxford: Peter Lang, 2012).

[10] CES, 2014. See press release welcoming changes to GCSE and GCE A-Level: http://www.catholiceducation.org.uk/news/ces-news (website last accessed on 03/01/18).

[11] In the Code of Canon Law (1983), Canon 803 provides the definition of a Catholic school, with Canon 803:3 stating that no school, even if it is Catholic, may use the title 'Catholic school' without the consent of the bishop. Canon 806:1 states the diocesan bishop has the right of supervision, visitation and inspection of Catholic schools in his diocese, even those established or directed by members of religious orders. He also has the right to issue directives concerning the general regulation of Catholic schools.

[12] In a number of dioceses, the local bishop has recognised these factors and given permission for some schools to study Islam rather than Judaism as the second religion. For example two schools in Salford diocese are in this position and one school in Arundel and Brighton.

[13] For a fuller discussion of this argument, Whittle (ed.), *Researching Catholic Education*, 237–238

[14] In October 2011, the CES (Catholic Education Service) launched a campaign to lobby the government to make RS GCSE one of the eligible subjects for the English Baccalaureate: http://www.catholiceducation.org.uk /news/ces-news/item/1002817-ces-campaign-for-the-inclusion-of-religious-education-in-exam-reforms (website last accessed 03/01/18).

[15] Such as Vatican II's, *Gravissimum Educationis* (1965). In: W. Abbott (ed., *The Documents of Vatican II* (New York: Herder and Herder, 1966).

[16] A. Casson, *Fragmented Catholicity and Social Cohesion: faith schools in a plural society* (Oxford: Peter Lang, 2012).

[17] K. Engebretson, *Catholic Schools and the Future of the Church* (London: Bloomsbury, 2014).

[18] Congregation for Catholic Education, *The Religious Dimension of Education in a Catholic School* (1988).

[19] S. Whittle, *A Theory of Catholic Education* (London: Bloomsbury, 2014).

[20] Currently 29.8% of pupils in Catholic schools and colleges in England are of other faiths and denominations or none. In Wales the figure is higher, where it is 42% of pupils. Source: Catholic Education Service (2015) Catholic education in England and Wales. Published on the CES website: http://www.catholiceducation.org.uk/ (website last accessed on 03/01/18).

[21] As the Vatican II document *Gravissimum Educationis* would put it.

[22] J. Conroy *et al.*, *Does Religious Education Work? A Multi-Dimensional Investigation* (London: Bloomsbury, 2013).

8 THE ROLE OF THE RE COORDINATOR IN CATHOLIC PRIMARY SCHOOLS IN ENGLAND

Sarah Nash

Sarah Nash has taught in Catholic primary schools in England for the past 23 years, of which she has spent 20 years as the RE coordinator in three different schools. As part of her role as RE coordinator she has also been on the senior leadership team in one of the schools.

Introduction

THE MAJOR ROLE for RE coordinators is to carry out and fulfil the Catholic mission set out for schools by the Church. The conciliar document on education sets out the importance of Catholic schools, it states:

> Among all educational instruments the school has a special importance. It is designed not only to develop with special care the intellectual faculties but also to form the ability to judge rightly, to hand on the cultural legacy of previous generations, to foster a sense of values, to prepare for professional life. Between pupils of different talents and backgrounds it promotes friendly relations and fosters a spirit of mutual understanding; and it establishes as it were a centre whose work and progress must be shared together by families, teachers, associations of various types that foster cultural, civic, and religious life, as well as by civil society and the entire human community.[1]

This clearly sets forward the distinctive mission of Catholic education whereby schools are expected to create environments where children achieve academically but that this is not the only aim of a Catholic education. Schools also need to develop pupil's consciences, allow them to develop a sense of values, prepare them for the world of work, fulfil the potential of pupils of all levels of ability and backgrounds, to renew the Catholic faith within a new generation and create rounded people who will benefit the whole of society. Again, during Pope Benedict XVI's visit to the United Kingdom in 2010, he addressed teachers saying:

> As you know, the task of a teacher is not simply to impart information or to provide training in skills intended to deliver some economic benefit to society; education is not and must never be considered as purely utilitarian. It is about forming the human person, equipping him or her to live life to the full—in short it is about imparting wisdom. And true wisdom is inseparable from knowledge of the Creator, for "both we and our words are in his hand, as are all understanding and skill in crafts (Ws 7:16).[2]

This chapter will seek to address what the role of the RE coordinator is within the mission of Catholic education in 'forming the whole person' and how this important role within Catholic Primary schools seeks to achieve this.

The Role of the RE Coordinator as Subject Leader

The role of the subject leader in schools has been defined by government, in which it states that:

> A subject leader provides leadership and direction for the subject and ensures that it is managed and organised to meet the aims and objectives of the school and the subject… Throughout their work, a subject leader ensures that practices improve the quality of education provided, meet the needs and aspirations of all pupils, and raise standards of achievement in the school… A subject leader plays a key role in supporting, guiding and motivating teachers of the subject, and other adults. Subject leaders evaluate the effectiveness of teaching and learning, the subject curriculum and progress towards targets for pupils and staff, to inform future priorities and targets for the subject. A

subject leader identifies needs in their own subject and recognises that these must be considered in relation to the overall needs of the school. It is important that a subject leader has an understanding of how their subject contributes to school priorities and to the overall education and achievement of all pupils.[3]

However, the Catholic education system, whilst agreeing with the above goes further by stating through the new directory for the religious education curriculum that RE coordinators should:

- be prepared to give living witness to what they teach;
- recognise that they share in the teaching office of the Church exercised in the person of the local bishop and enshrined in the trust deed of the school;
- fulfil their professional responsibilities with regard to all that develops and enhances the life of the Catholic school;
- plan and teach schemes of work that are engaging and accessible so that all pupils may progress appropriately in their knowledge and understanding of the Catholic faith;
- have high expectations of all their pupils;
- ensure that 10% of the curriculum to age 16 and 5% of the curriculum beyond the age of 16 is devoted to Religious Education;
- ensure that Religious Education contributes positively to the broad and balanced curriculum of a Catholic school through cooperation and dialogue with other subjects.[4]

This significant qualitative difference focuses on the phrase 'be prepared to give living witness'. The role has been expanded upon by many of the dioceses within England and Wales who have created their own documents about the roles and responsibilities of RE coordinators. Southwark Archdiocese, for instance, reflects the Curriculum directory but also includes organising training for other members of staff, selecting and purchasing resources to enhance RE teaching, and ensure that RE is planned for, monitored and evaluated. Another diocese, that of Hexham and Newcastle, includes liaising with the Diocesan Department of Education, inducting new members of staff with the mission of the school and the RE scheme of work and to set up and maintain a portfolio of work. Finally, Hallam diocese also states that the role of the RE coordinator should include leading staff in a time of reflection before each new topic is taught to the pupils, as well as work with the senior leadership team to undertake a regular review of Religious Education in line with the school development plan.

The Role of the RE Coordinator as a Christian Ministry

The role of the RE coordinator can only be achieved if the person who is appointed is fully committed to the mission and faith life of the school. As a result of this: 'the Head Teacher, Deputy Head Teacher and RE Coordinator must be practising Catholics'.[5]

As a practising Catholic, therefore, the role of the RE coordinator is to set an example to pupils and colleagues, to model Christian ministry, to encourage and help staff who are not Catholic in their ability to teach the faith and to live out the gospel values in their relationships with pupils, parents, staff and parish as well as through the way they teach. In the Catholic Bishops Conference of 2000, the Bishops stated that:

> RE teaching in a Catholic school will be enlightened by the faith of the school community and by the faith of the RE teacher. Its educational focus will be formed and enhanced by the vitality of faith. For some in the classroom, religious education may well be received as catechesis, deepening and enhancing their personal faith; for some it will be evangelisation, the first time they will have been presented, personally, with the truths of living faith.[6]

It is through their faith and witness that others are brought to a closer relationship with Christ. In addition, the centrality of the sacramental perspective, that is all ministries especially RE coordinators, should be modelled on that of Christ, must greatly affect this role. In practice this means that teachers should be dedicated to Jesus' style of ministry, encompassing concepts such as invitation and inclusion. John Lydon states that:

> By engaging in the ministry of teaching, the individual Christian is responding to his or her primary call to be a disciple of Jesus, in a distinctive manner, reflecting the notion of charisms being a concrete realisation of the universal gift of God through Christ to all the baptised ... This fundamental calling demands that all teachers model their ministry on that of Christ. Teachers are, in effect, signs of the presence of Christ within their educational communities.[7]

It is through RE coordinators' witness that they fulfil their sacramental duty, by acting in a certain way they are serving the next generation of Catholics.

The Role of the RE Coordinator to Liaise with the SLT

The RE coordinator also needs to be empowered by the leadership and governors so that they can ensure that religious teaching is the foundation and a core subject of the curriculum. As a consequence, the RE coordinator needs to work with other subject leaders to make sure that the Catholic faith underpins all that is taught. The National Board of Religious Inspectors and Advisors state that:

> The task of linking learning across subjects is not easy and staff need help to make connections for themselves and for their pupils. For example, staff teaching science and religious education should be aware of each other's work and be conscious of the questions that will arise. In history, geography and sport, staff should know and have a common attitude to human development and skills, regard for the human body and for global responsibility... More than that, such discussions can lead to a greater under-

standing of what is involved in educating for the spiritual
and moral development of young people.[8]

As a result, if an RE coordinator works closely with all staff,
especially those who are not Catholic, but particularly with
subject leaders and is able to ensure that ten percent of curriculum time is dedicated to the teaching of RE, then they will be
fulfilling their role of making sure that RE is the central feature
of the curriculum.

A major part of the role of any subject leader is the need to be
able to work closely with Head Teachers and members of the
leadership team in order to fulfil their role:

> ... the major challenge is about head teacher and classroom
> colleagues wanting coordinators to have a substantive role,
> and trusting them to carry it out. The former needs head
> teachers to delegate authority and responsibility to coor-
> dinators and to endorse publically the role. The latter
> requires coordinators to demonstrate that they can help
> individual colleagues to improve teaching and learning in
> the curriculum area.[9]

The standards for subject leaders states that in working with the
senior leadership team, coordinators need to keep them informed
about the levels of achievement within their subject, what the areas
for improvement are and how these could be achieved so that
leadership can make informed decisions which should be included
in the whole school development program. However, as RE
coordinator within a Catholic school context this role needs to be
taken further. RE coordinators should help the head teacher to
fulfil the mission of the school and make sure that the distinctive
nature of Catholic Education is upheld within it. The document
'What is different about being a middle manager in a Catholic
school' states that the role of the subject coordinator will:

• Secure the contribution of the subject to a curriculum where
  high standards and the dignity of the individual pupil and
  members of staff are promoted;

- Support the growth of a community in which the quality of relationships demonstrates commitment to gospel values;
- Ensure that, in all areas, priority is given to the spiritual, moral, social and cultural development of pupils and staff;
- Develop strategies, procedures and day to day routines which put into practice the mission of the school.[10]

In this way the RE coordinator works together with the Head Teacher to ensure that the distinctive nature of Catholic Education is maintained and promoted within the school and parish. The Catholic ethos of the school should pervade every subject, activity and relationship. This cannot be achieved by one person alone and therefore the senior leadership team need to work closely with the RE coordinator to ensure that this happens through reviewing policies together, through training of staff, through staff focused as well as pupil focused retreats, liturgies and so on, constant review of how the school is showing it's Catholic values outwardly as well as inwardly and through the relationships and community spirit that is created. The new directory for the religious education curriculum states that:

> The presentation of the Christian message influences the way in which, for example, the origins of the world, the sense of history, the basis of ethical values, the function of religion in culture, the destiny of the human person, and our relationship with nature, are understood. Religious Education in schools underpins, activates, develops and completes the educational and catechetical activity of the whole school.[11]

Therefore the main way that RE coordinators promote the distinctive mission of a Catholic Primary school is to work closely with the leadership team, staff, parents, clergy and pupils to ensure that Catholic values and beliefs pervade every area of school life and put Christ at the Centre of our educational endeavour.

Challenges Faced by RE coordinators in Fulfilling their Role

There are many challenges that RE coordinators face in achieving their goals. The first of which is the tension of being a middle manager:

> They find themselves mediating between, on the one hand, the 'front line' perspective of the classroom teacher whose main priority is coping with pupils and survival on a day to day basis, and, on the other hand, the whole school context and longer term perspective constantly brought home to them by senior staff.[12]

Consequently, the RE coordinator needs to work together with the Head Teacher and staff to ensure that the distinctive nature of Catholic Education is maintained and promoted within the school and parish and should pervade every subject, activity and relationship. The RE coordinator should therefore be on the Senior Leadership Team to ensure that this happens through reviewing policies, through training of staff, through staff focused as well as pupil focused retreats, liturgies and so on constant review of how the school is showing it's Catholic values outwardly as well as inwardly and through the relationships and community spirit that is created. The problem faced by RE coordinators in Primary schools is that they are often not part of the Senior Leadership Team; they are viewed as middle managers, and can therefore struggle to get their voice heard and effect change.

Another tension could be the impact of market values, which in educational terms can be seen as academic achievement as the only measure of success of a school. James Arthur states that:

> The danger is that to focus on examination success is to view only one element of schooling that may lead many to take this one measurement as evidence of the overall standard of performance in the wider, more diffuse process

of Catholic schooling. Whilst a measurable performance indicator is a useful tool, it is not in itself evidence of achieving the aims of catholic schooling—which is to provide a Catholic educational experience and formation.[13]

Although academic achievement is a primary aim of Catholic schooling it is not seen as the only measure of success and herein could lay the tension. Catholic educational principles also uphold the need to develop the whole person, develop their spirituality and relationship with God, develop their morality and ability to make well founded decisions, to develop their understanding of their place in society and be able to contribute to it.

Another tension is developing the spirituality of pupils within the Catholic education system and Catholic schools actually following their mission statements of providing an education based on the gospel values. The pressure on leaders and coordinators to constantly introduce new initiatives, to fill out paperwork, to constantly assess children and adjust planning accordingly can lead to a stressed workforce which filters down to the pupils. The requirement and duty of schools to provide the time and space to develop pupils spirituality can be pushed to one side with the pressures of the secular curriculum. Catholic schools should have daily acts of worship, allow children to attend Mass and the Sacraments on a regular basis, give them a place to pray and be quiet whenever they need it, as well as support them on their spiritual journey of faith. This can be a challenge when league table positions need to be high in order to be considered a successful school:

> Head teachers indicated that, in a competitive marketplace in which schools are being judged exclusively on academic achievement, they are challenged by parents and children who do not appreciate gospel values. Catholic schools aim to educate future generations in the traditions of the Church and teachers who work in these schools strive to provide an education that is more comprehensive then that measured by narrow league table results. There is a

challenge to uphold spiritual values in a culture where
league tables are emphasised.[14]

The secular education system can appear not to reflect the gospel
values such as compassion, humility, justice, forgiveness, tolerance and peace which all Catholic schools should be promoting,
and it can appear to strive merely for individual perfection in
academic achievement with little regard for society as a whole.
This is the challenge RE coordinators and Head Teachers face,
to live with, and actively promote Gospel values in all that
happens within the school when pressure is applied to constantly
improve academic results.

The Vatican document states that:

> Prime responsibility for creating this unique Christian
> school climate rests with the teachers, as individuals and
> as a community. The religious dimension of the school
> climate is expressed through the celebration of Christian
> values in Word and Sacrament, in individual behaviour,
> in friendly and harmonious interpersonal relationships,
> and in a ready availability. Through this daily witness, the
> students will come to appreciate the uniqueness of the
> environment to which their youth has been entrusted. If
> it is not present, then there is little left which can make the
> school Catholic.[15]

Therefore, RE coordinators need to be on the senior leadership
team, so that the many tensions and pressures, do not water down
or dissolve the distinctive mission of Catholic schools.

Conclusion

In conclusions the role of the RE coordinator should be held by
a practising Catholic who takes a lead role in teaching the faith,
organising masses, sacraments and assemblies, but also is there
to set an example to pupils and colleagues, to model Christian
ministry, to encourage and help staff who are not Catholic in their
ability to teach the faith and to live out the gospel values in their

relationships with pupils, parents, staff and parish as well as through the way they teach.

Finally, the role of the RE coordinator not only encompasses RE teaching but development of faith, spirituality and Christian ministry and therefore the role needs to be held by a practising Catholic, who has a clear understanding of their faith. Also, if the distinctive mission of Catholic education is going to be upheld then it is necessary for the RE coordinator to have a strategic role in the leadership of the school and be seen by the whole community as a leader who is able to effect change.

Notes

1. Vatican Council II, *Gravissimum Educationis* – Declaration on Christian Education (1965), 5.
2. Pope Benedict XVI, *Address to Teachers and Religious, Chapel of St Mary's University College*, Twickenham, UK (2010), 2.
3. Teacher Training Agency (TTA), *National Standards for Subject Leaders* (London: TTA, 1998), 4.
4. Catholic Bishops' Conference of England and Wales (CBCEW), *Religious Education Curriculum Directory* (London: Catholic Education Service, 2012), 5.
5. Rev. M. Stock, *Christ at the Centre, Diocesan Schools Commission* (Archdiocese of Birmingham, 2005), 5.
6. Catholic Bishops' Conference of England and Wales, *Religious Education in Catholic Schools* (London: Catholic Media Office, 2000), 8.
7. J. Lydon, *The Contemporary Catholic Teacher: A Reappraisal of the Concept of Teaching as a Vocation in the Catholic Christian Context* (Saarbrucken, Germany: Lambert Academic Publishing, 2011), 160.
8. National Board of Religious Inspectors and Advisors (NBRIA), *The Distinctive Curriculum of a Catholic School: Guidelines for School Review* (Luton, 2012), 8.
9. J. O'Neill, 'The Role of the Co-ordinator'. In: J. O'Neill & N. Kitson, *Effective Curriculum Management: Co-ordinating Learning in a Primary School* (London and New York: Routledge, 1996), 20–31.
10. Catholic Education Service (CES), *What is different about being a middle manager in a Catholic School?* (London: CES, 1999), A7.
11. Catholic Bishops' Conference of England and Wales (CBCEW), *Religious Education Curriculum Directory* (London: Catholic Education Service,

2012), 4.

[12]   J. Sullivan, 'Leadership and Management'. In: M.A. Hayes & L. Gearon (eds), *Contemporary Catholic Education* (Leominster: Gracewing, 2002), 98.

[13]   J. Arthur, 'Measuring Catholic School Performance'. In: R. Gardner, J. Cairns, & D. Lawton, *Faith Schools: Consensus or Conflict* (London: Routledge, 2005), 152–153.

[14]   D. Fincham, 'Headteachers in Catholic Schools: challenges of leadership', *International Studies in Catholic Education*, Vol. 2/No. 1 (Spring 2010), 70.

[15]   Congregation for Catholic Education, *The Religious Dimension of Education in a Catholic School* (1988), 26.

9 CHAPLAINCY AND RELIGIOUS DIVERSITY

Teresa Lucas

Teresa Lucas has worked for eight years as lay Chaplain at a Catholic independent school in England, having previously worked at a residential retreat centre for young people. She has an MA in Pastoral Theology from St. Mary's University Twickenham and an MA in Theology from Oxford University.

Introduction

IN THIS CHAPTER I aim to explore how the ministry of a Catholic School Chaplain[1] may be meaningfully undertaken within the context of a religiously diverse student body, and to consider how this relates to the Church's teaching both on the proclamation of the gospel and dialogue with those of other faiths. It is written in light of my own experiences as a lay Chaplain in a Catholic school in England for students aged 11–18. This school has a student body made up of less than 40% Catholics, and it is this which has led me to reflect on whether ministry to a religiously diverse student body should be seen as a problem to be tackled, a challenge to be embraced or an opportunity to be enjoyed, and on how a Chaplain can and should balance both proclamation and dialogue.

In order to consider this question, let us begin by reflecting on the Church's teaching on religious diversity, specifically interfaith dialogue, its place in the Church's mission and its relationship to proclamation.

The Church and Religious Diversity

Over the last fifty years, the Church has more clearly articulated the nature of her relationship with those of other faiths. A Vatican

II document stated that the Church 'rejects nothing of what is true and holy' in other religions[2], pointed to the common origin and destiny of humanity[3], and urged the faithful to 'enter with prudence and charity into discussion and collaboration with members of other religions'.[4] In 1990 Pope Saint John Paul II stated that 'inter-religious dialogue is a part of the Church's evangelising mission[5] and, more recently, Pope Francis has written that 'inter-religious dialogue is a necessary condition for peace in the world, and so it is a duty for Christians as well as other religious communities'.[6]

The Church's teaching on interfaith dialogue has been outlined in two documents.[7] It stated that the two goals of interreligious dialogue are mutual understanding and mutual enrichment[8] and highlighted four types of dialogue. The first is the Dialogue of Life whereby people of different faiths live together sharing each other's 'joys and sorrows'.[9] This is not simply co-existence but something which 'requires openness, a desire to enter into relations with others'.[10] The second is the Dialogue of Action through which people of different faiths work together to promote issues such as peace, justice and the environment. Next there is the Dialogue of Theological Exchange 'where specialists seek to deepen their understanding of their respective religious heritages'.[11] Finally there is the Dialogue of Religious Experience 'where persons rooted in their own religious traditions share their spiritual riches, for instance with regard to prayer and contemplation, faith and ways of searching for God or the Absolute'.[12] These four types of dialogue make clear that, 'dialogue is not so much an idea to be studied as a way of living in positive relationship with others'[13], a fact exemplified by the occasions on which he met with and prayed alongside leaders of other faiths, actions which have been continued by both his successors.

How though, does the Church's call to dialogue relate to the mandate to proclaim Christ? The answer is that both dialogue and proclamation are seen as 'authentic elements of the Church's evangelising mission'.[14] Dialogue is a part of evangelisation because evangelisation is much wider than the explicit proclamation of Jesus and the call to conversion[15], central though this is. Thus proclamation and dialogue are 'intimately related, but not interchangeable'[16] and are both elements of the Church's evangelising mission.

It is possible to see, however, that these two elements of proclamation and dialogue might be difficult to balance; it is easy to see how one might overshadow the other and how a certain 'tension' may arise between the two, particularly within the context of a Catholic school.

The Mission of the Catholic School

The Congregation for Catholic Education makes clear that the fact that Christ is the foundation and centre of the whole 'educational enterprise' in a Catholic school, and the fact that the school aims to develop the whole person, gives the Catholic school its distinctively Catholic character.[17] Thus the Catholic Education Service of England and Wales (CES) writes that the mission of the Catholic school 'will always be centred on Christ, reflect a Christian understanding of the purpose of education, and make explicit the Christian values and principles by which the school operates'.[18] In addition, in the years since Vatican II, the mission and distinctive nature of a Catholic school have come to be seen as ones which include a positive relationship and dialogue with students of other faiths. In England and Wales, this is particularly seen in the CES's 2008 document, which emphasises the responsibility which Catholic schools have to students of other faiths and the contribution they make to the Catholic school.[19]

Pope Benedict XVI, in his address to students in Catholic schools in Great Britain at the 'Big Assembly' during his 2010 UK visit, especially addressed non-Catholic students saying:

> I know that there are many non-Catholics studying in the Catholic Schools in Great Britain, and I wish to include all of you in my words today...You are a reminder to them [Catholic students] of the bigger picture that exists outside

the school, and indeed, it is only right that respect and friendship for members of other religious traditions should be among the virtues learned in a Catholic school.[20]

The key point is that the Catholic school needs to be both confident in living out its distinctly Catholic identity and confident in engaging in dialogue.[21] Indeed, engaging in dialogue is part of its Catholic identity.

The Ministry of the School Chaplain

For the School Chaplain, then, an important part of his or her ministry will be the daily need to balance both proclamation of the gospel and dialogue with those of other faiths. The witness of the Chaplain's own life will be a significant part of this as well; for this witness to be authentic, just as the school needs to be confident in both proclamation of the gospel and dialogue, so also the School Chaplain. The Chaplain is called to be someone rooted in Christ and in the prayer life of the Church, someone who recognises their own faith journey and is willing to walk with others on theirs, wherever it may take them, and to be humbled by the experience.[22] Equally, the Chaplain is called to recognise the value of dialogue with those of other faiths and not be afraid to enter into it; something which requires courage, a willingness to acknowledge when mistakes may be made, and an openness to the 'other' and to Christ.[23] This Church document recognises that interfaith dialogue is not easy and that there are a number of obstacles to dialogue, including a lack of confidence on the part of one or both of the dialogue partners.[24] It is especially important, therefore, that School Chaplains, as well as RE teachers and school leadership teams, are given support in the area of providing for students and staff of other faiths whilst maintaining the Catholic identity of the school.

Whilst the School Chaplain has a unique and privileged role to play in the living out of the school's Catholic mission, it is the responsibility of all staff to ensure this mission is embodied in the daily life of the school. Thus, the Chaplain should aim to engage the entire school community in the task of proclamation and dialogue. Above all, however, the Chaplain is called to offer his or her ministry back to God, and to ask him to work through both the Chaplain's mistakes and successes to bring people into a closer relationship with God himself.

Chaplaincy: Proclamation and Dialogue—Some Examples

How then can a School Chaplain balance the need for proclamation of the Christian message with the need for dialogue?

First, let us consider proclamation. A clear proclamation of Christ can be given through the celebrations of Mass and the other Sacraments, the celebration of liturgical seasons, other times of prayer, such as the rosary and Stations of the Cross, and retreats. There may also be opportunities for ongoing formation for Catholic students, for example through preparation to become an Extraordinary Minister of Holy Communion, and attendance at local and national Catholic events such as, in England and Wales, the Catholic Youth Ministry Federation (CYMFed) Flame Conferences.

The Chaplain will proclaim Christ through the pastoral care he or she shows to students and staff, and by providing opportunities for students to put their faith into action through community service. There will also be the physical signs of the Catholic Christian faith such as the Chapel, crucifixes and statues.

Second, let us consider dialogue using the four types outlined above. Within the specific realms of Chaplaincy, the dialogue of life, people of different faiths actively living alongside each other, will be fostered through the various ways in which the Chaplain supports all students as they study and, in the case of boarding schools, live, alongside and in close proximity to those of other faiths and learn how to do so in a neighbourly way. This in effect allows students to enter into a dialogue of life in an unforced way.

Equally, the Chaplain will foster a dialogue of life as they work with all staff in creating an environment in which each person is helped to grow more fully into the person God is calling them to be, and by providing opportunities for people to share and pray for the 'joys and sorrows' of others in the community each day.

Most students and staff would probably not realise that these things can be viewed as a form of interfaith dialogue. How far this lack of consciousness may be a problem in need of addressing is debateable. On the one hand, not realising that one is participating in a form of dialogue does not mean that the dialogue is not taking place or is any less meaningful. On the other hand, older students and staff could perhaps gain more from an increased consciousness of the value of being part of a religiously plural community in a Catholic setting, and of a realisation that in such a community people of many faiths and none can work alongside each other, journeying towards a common goal, respecting each other and deepening their own relationship with God. Education in dialogue must be age appropriate; care should be taken that students younger in their Catholic faith are not confused by calls to dialogue, yet the reality is that many students—young and older—are part of a religiously plural school (and wider) community and should be helped to understand and engage with this. For older students, a workshop can be included, either within a retreat or programme of faith formation, which looks at the question of being a Catholic in today's religiously plural world and the value of interfaith dialogue. Careful preparation is needed before this sort of activity but if all are open to the discussion, it can be a fruitful time. For the youngest students simply being invited to be an active and valued part of the school community is the start of this learning process.

The 'dialogue of justice' can be fostered by the Chaplain each time they enable and encourage students and staff of all faiths to undertake, together, some form of community service—faith in action. As part of this, it may be possible to share something of the call all faiths make to work for justice, to acknowledge that those serving the community come from many faith backgrounds but are all working for the same end, and to explain how this is a form of dialogue.

It is primarily within the context of Religious Studies or Religious Education lessons that any formal 'dialogue of theological exchange' may take place within a school, as students undertake units of work concerned with the major religions of the world whilst maintaining a focus on Christianity, and Catholicism in particular. The role of the Chaplain within this will vary between schools.

Now we turn to the fourth kind of dialogue, that of religious experience, which is perhaps the most complicated to maintain within the daily life of a Catholic school. The Chaplain is faced with the question of how to best animate the prayer life of the school so that as many members of the community as possible feel able to approach God in prayer, and so that there is a real sense of being a community who prays together. At the same time, the Chaplain must avoid syncretism[25] and religious relativism, and consider the guidelines provided by the various bodies which inspect the school.

One way forward is to make space within the school's rhythm of prayer for times of collective silent reflection and prayer, following John Paul II's example when he invited faith leaders to meet in Assisi to join together in praying for peace.[26] In my own school we have attempted this in our own small way at our annual Thanksgiving Day non-Eucharistic Liturgy. In the weeks before Thanksgiving, students and staff are invited to volunteer to represent their faith community by reading a thanksgiving prayer at the Service. Towards the end of this Liturgy everyone is invited to listen to the prayers and then join in a time of silence which follows. Given the school context, the time of silence is not very long but there is always a noticeable atmosphere of prayer throughout the congregation and those who lead the prayers are a witness to the whole school community of the strength and diversity of faith within that community. A similar sharing of reflection, prayer and silence, has been entered into on the theme of peace for the United Nations Interfaith Harmony Week.

It can also be helpful to reflect on the way the school's daily morning prayer is structured. In my own school, we have decided to prepare the morning prayer so that as many people as possible feel able to make it their own. If the focus of the reflection is a religious festival, either a Christian feast day or a major festival of another world religion, then the key themes, for example, forgiveness, celebration, light are highlighted together with their relevance to daily life. Students are invited either to discuss the theme as a group or to reflect quietly on this in relation to their own lives. After a moment of reflection, the concluding prayer will be read. This prayer does not usually include the Trinitarian formula but is addressed to 'Loving God'. This is not so that we can avoid proclaiming Christ in order to smooth out differences but rather, because we feel that in the context of a school with a religiously diverse student population, it is both appropriate and necessary to provide moments of reflection and prayer which are accessible to as many people as possible, since it has a responsibility to aid the spiritual development of all. Often it is appropriate, as mentioned above, to gather for silent prayer but there is arguably huge value in, once a day, having a voiced prayer which many students, not only our Christian students, feel able to make their own. However, the reason we feel this is appropriate, is because we are confident in our proclamation of Christ and feel that we provide many other experiences of prayer which are more explicitly Christocentric.

Conclusion

The Church's mission to proclaim the good news and the Church's call to enter into dialogue with those of other faiths are both 'authentic elements of the Church's evangelising mission'.[27] It is necessary, therefore, for a Chaplain working within a Catholic school with a religiously plural student body to maintain a 'healthy balance' between proclaiming the Gospel and engaging in interfaith dialogue; the two need to be held 'in tension' since they are intimately connected but not interchangeable[28] and neither should supersede the other. Proclamation and dialogue for a School Chaplain is about proclaiming in words and actions the faith of Christ Jesus and welcoming those of other faiths, walking with them in their faith journey, learning with and from them. However, whilst the presence in some Catholic schools of a large number of non-Catholic students may have brought the question of how a Chaplain should minister to a religiously diverse student population to the forefront in recent years, it is the fact that dialogue is a key part of the Church's mission which should be the real cause for a Chaplain to reflect on his or her ministry in this light. The question of dialogue with those of other faiths, then, is one which should be addressed by all School Chaplains and not only those in schools with a large number of non-Catholic students.

The task of maintaining the balance between proclamation and dialogue in a Catholic school is, for a School Chaplain, therefore at once a challenge and an opportunity. As a challenge it brings with it responsibility and requires courage. As an opportunity it should be seized because in dialoguing as well as proclaiming, we learn, we draw closer to Christ and closer to each other, and we enable others to do the same; this is the task of the Catholic school, the vocation of all who work in them, and the ministry of the School Chaplain.

Notes

[1]   According to Canon 564, only a priest may be called 'Chaplain', however many School Chaplains in England and Wales are now lay people. For ease of expression, the title 'School Chaplain' when used in this chapter will refer to lay, religious and ordained Chaplains.

[2]   Vatican II, *Nostra Aetate* – Declaration on the Relation of the Church to Non-Christian Religions (1965), 2.

[3]   *Ibid.,* 1.

4   *Ibid.,* 2.

5   Pope St John Paul II, *Redemptoris Missio* – on the permanent validity of the Church's missionary mandate, (1990), 5.

6   Pope Francis, Apostolic Exhortation *Evangelii Gaudium* – on the proclamation of the gospel in today's world, (2013), 250.

7   The Pontifical Council for Inter-Religious Dialogue outlined the Church's teaching on interfaith dialogue in *Dialogue and Mission (DM)* in 1984 and *Dialogue and Proclamation (DP)* in 1991.

8   *Ibid., DP,* 9

9   Cf. Vatican II, *Gaudium et spes* – The Pastoral Constitution on the Church in the Modern World (1965), 1.

10   M. L. Fitzgerald, *The Catholic Church and Interreligious Dialogue,* paper given at a workshop for American Benedictine Abbots held at the Prince of Peace Benedictine Monastery in Oceanside, California, January 2005.

11   The Pontifical Council for Inter-religious Dialogue, *DP* (1991), 42.

12   *Ibid.,* 42.

13   Pope St John Paul II, *Address to the Pontifical Council for Interreligious Dialogue,* 26 April 1990, cited by Catholic Bishops' Conference of England and Wales, *Meeting God in Friend and Stranger* (London: Catholic Truth Society, 2010), 2.

14   The Pontifical Council for Inter-religious Dialogue, *DP* (1991), 77.

15   Catholic Bishops' Conference of England and Wales, *Meeting God in Friend and Stranger,* 86.

16   The Pontifical Council for Inter-religious Dialogue, *DP* (1991), 77.

17   Congregation for Catholic Education, *The Catholic School* (1977), 34; 35.

18   Catholic Education Service for England and Wales, *Evaluating the Distinctive Nature of a Catholic school* (London: Catholic Education Service, 1999), A–11.

19   Catholic Education Service, *Catholic Schools, Children of Other Faiths and Community Cohesion: Cherishing Education for Human Growth* (London: CES, 2008).

20   Pope Benedict XVI, *Address to Pupils, St. Mary's University College, Twickenham, England* (2010).

21   As described in The Pontifical Council's for Inter-religious Dialogue, *DP* (1991).

22   M. A. Hayes, 'The Disposition of the Chaplain'. In: M. A. Hayes & L. Gearon (eds) *Contemporary Catholic Education* (Leominster: Gracewing, 2002), 134.

23   The Pontifical Council for Inter-Religious Dialogue, *DP* (1991), 47–49.

24   *Ibid.,* 52.

25 Catholic Bishops' Conference of England and Wales, *Meeting God in Friend and Stranger*, 152.
26 *Ibid.*, 152.
27 The Pontifical Council for Inter-Religious Dialogue, *DP* (1991), 77.
28 *Ibid.*, 77.

PART III:
LEADERSHIP AND
GOVERNANCE

Five International Challenges: An Analysis for Governors, Headteachers and Teachers to Discuss and Take Action

Professor Gerald Grace

Professor Gerald Grace KSG is the Director of the Centre for Research and Development in Catholic Education (CRDCE) at St. Mary's University, Twickenham, London. He founded the journal, 'International Studies in Catholic Education' (ISCE) in March 2009 and is the Executive Editor.

School Self-Evaluation: an Important Complement to Government Evaluation

THE PRINCIPAL OF Holy Family School, Parktown, South Africa and the Headmaster of Sacred Heart College, Johannesburg have both witnessed to the value of this activity in their recent article.[1] The conclusion of their research report, 'that colleague-implemented school evaluation was far more desirable and effective than State-mandated school inspection systems'[2] sends an important message to all Catholic schools and colleges and it also provides the theoretical framework for this chapter.[3]

While government mandated inspection systems have a necessary role to play in monitoring the effectiveness of teaching, learning and discipline in schools and in providing accountability evidence for public authorities and for parents, the criteria which they use represent only one dimension of the life of a school. The dominant criteria used are secular measures of performance effectiveness (as measured by tests and examination results) and of compliance with legislative requirements and existing regulations. This may be called *Performative Secular Evaluation (PSEV)*. The prime focus of government external inspectors is therefore concerned with the technical effectiveness and bureaucratic compliance of the school, its measured efficiency. It is the evaluation of an institution.

However for Catholic schools and colleges a second (and equally important) form of evaluation is needed which may be called Mission Catholic Evaluation (MCEV). The prime focus of MCEV is concerned with a larger perspective related to issues such as the vitality of Catholicity and spirituality in the school, its mission integrity, its distinctive mode of leadership, the extent to which Catholic Religious and Social Teaching is part of its educational programme and how its overall culture and ethos facilitates a process of integral formation for its students and not just a process of training. It is the evaluation of a distinctive mission.

As international research studies have shown,[4] in the context of a globalised and increasingly marketised world, the operative influence of *PSEV* forms of evaluation in education is becoming stronger in conditions of global economic competition.[5] The consequences of this have the potential to colonise the relatively autonomous mission cultures of Catholic schools as the requirements for *PSEV* become also the dominant concern of Catholic school and college leaders. Part of the problem is that *PSEV* is empowered by external and influential teams of government inspectors. In most countries, *MCEV* lacks such powerful resources and as a consequence is in danger of being marginalised in discussions of school 'effectiveness' and even in the consciousness and discourse of Catholic School leaders.[6] Mission distinctiveness becomes problematic.

One obvious defence for Catholic educational institutions internationally to utilise in this situation of potential ideological incorporation is the practice of school self evaluation using the colleague-implemented approaches.[7]

Mission Catholic Evaluation could be undertaken by colleague teams within the school working in partnership with colleague teams external to the school as monitors, for example, recently retired Catholic school leaders and teachers. In this way, Catholic schools and colleges could insist that any judgements about the 'effectiveness' of their institutions would have to be based upon the formula, $PSEV + MCEV$ = Catholic school effectiveness.[8]

Mission Catholic Evaluation: an Agenda of 5 Challenges

It is clear that colleague professionals involved in the undertaking of self-evaluation will need to operate with the same standards of impartiality and objectivity used by external government inspectors. However, unlike most secular inspectors, these colleagues will need to possess a good understanding of the fundamental principles which characterise the Catholic educational mission.

In particular this will involve the ability to assess and evaluate the various manifestations of a school's Catholicity and of its mission integrity. This mode of evaluation ($MCEV$) is more comprehensively cultural, social and values-based than the technical/bureaucratic mode represented by $PSEV$.

Just as $PSEV$ inspectors operate with a check-list of issues and categories to be observed and evaluated, colleague professionals will require an agenda of issues to be investigated and the following Schema is suggested as one possible template for this process.

a. The Vitality of Catholicity and Spirituality in the School: (VCS criterion)[9]

An authoritative statement from the Congregation for Catholic Education in its 1977 publication, has established very clearly what has to be the first priority criterion in any Mission Catholic Evaluation exercise. This is declared in two paragraphs, that is:

> Christ is the foundation of the whole educational enterprise in a Catholic school.[10]
> Mindful of the fact that man has been redeemed by Christ, the Catholic school aims at forming in the Christian those

> particular virtues which will enable him to live a new life
> in Christ.[11]

These foundational educational aims provoke the question, what does this mean in educational practice?

While the realisation of these aims will obviously vary in individual school cultures, certain common indicators of the Catholicity of schools will exist. These will include a ring-fenced allocation of time and resources for Religious Education;[12] the services of a Chaplain in secondary schools and the regular presence of the local parish priest in primary schools; regular celebration of Mass and other liturgies in the school and nearby churches and preparation of pupils and students for the initiatory rites of the Church (first Holy Communion and Confirmation). At the same time, the Life and Teachings of Jesus Christ will be a central feature of the curriculum programme of the school, not only in Religious Education, but permeated in various ways in other teaching subjects as occasions arise.[13] The provision of a 'sacred place' within the school, either in the form of a chapel or a simple prayer and meditation/mindfulness room will be an indicator that the school takes the spiritual nurture of its students seriously, along with opportunities for Retreat experiences for both staff and students.

Aware that post-Vatican II Catholic schools may have a significant presence of students of other faiths, the Vatican document on education (1977) required all schools to make sensitive and respectful provision for those of other faiths:

> In the certainty that the Spirit is at work in every person,
> the Catholic school offers itself to all, non-Christians
> included ... acknowledging, preserving and promoting the
> spiritual and moral qualities, the social and cultural values
> which characterise different civilisations.[14]

From this more inclusive perspective, in contemporary conditions of 'the materialism, pragmatism and technocracy of society',[15] Catholic schools are expected to nurture not only the habitus of spirituality in the Catholic tradition, but other forms of spirituality having other sources of inspiration.[16] In other words, the Catholic school should be a creative centre for the cultivation of the spiritual potential of young people as well as their intellectual potential.

It cannot be expected, because of local resource and staffing constraints, that all Catholic schools can realise all of these VCS criteria—it is obviously an ideal-type profile. However, colleague professionals engaged in Mission Catholic Evaluation projects may, with sensitivity, find some of these criteria useful in assessing school 'effectiveness' in an alternative paradigm which takes spirituality seriously.

b. Mission Integrity (M.I. Criterion)

All Catholic schools will have mission statements which declare at the highest level the school's commitments to religious, moral, social, personal and educational principles and values. Such statements represent a *covenant* with the local community which says, in effect, this is the basis upon which you can judge us. *Mission integrity* can be defined as *'fidelity in practice, and not just in public rhetoric, to the distinctive and authentic principles of a Catholic education'*. It is the promises of the school's Mission Statement made manifest in its everyday educational life and practises.

A central focus of *MCEV* projects will therefore involve assessments of the extent to which a school is actually living out its mission commitments. Schools which achieve this can be seen to demonstrate high levels of mission integrity.

The challenge for all Catholic schools is to try to avoid the opposite pole of this spectrum, which is *Mission drift*. This may be defined as *'the generally unintentional drift from mission commitments over time, as a result of a complex of factors including social and political pressures and weak school leadership'*. The challenge for Catholic school leaders (headteachers and governors) is to maintain the necessary balance between 'Rendering to Caesar' (the State) and 'Rendering to God' in educational practice. In the contexts of contemporary globalisation the problem is that the Caesar/State in constantly increasing its demands for measurable 'output' from the schools.[17]

c. Commitments to the Common Good in Education (CG criterion)

One of the best statements of Catholic social values in education was made by the Catholic Bishops of England and Wales in their 1997 publication on education. The Bishops declared:

> No school or college is 'an island entire of itself'. It means that no Governing Body, no individual group of parents has the right to disregarded the good of another institution, while promoting the good of its own school of college.[18]

At the time when competitive market relations among schools in the UK were at their height after decades of influence from Neo-Liberalism[19] and other New Right ideologies, this declaration was entirely counter—cultural to a dominant market culture in education which encouraged individual schools to look to their individual market interests, as the prime focus.

The challenge for Catholic schools clearly stated by the English Bishops in 1997 is still relevant to Catholic schools internationally, that is:

> Popular and successful schools should explore ways of working in solidarity with those that are struggling, and in particular, with those serving deprived neighbourhoods.[20]

Mission Catholic Evaluation projects in popular and successful schools should therefore focus upon the extent to which the schools are demonstrating solidarity with disadvantaged schools. This may not be on the check-list of government inspectors but it will surely be an indicator that Catholic Social Teaching is being realised in educational practice.

d. A Distinctive Form of Catholic School Leadership (CSL criterion)

In recent decades internationally various attempts have been made to transform the position known as school principal, rector or headteacher (especially in the Secondary sector) to some form of Executive Director of an educational corporation, or what one academic[21] has described as *Education plc.* This has been one of the consequences of the attempted application of market principles and practices to educational institutions.

This conception of school leadership as primarily an organisational director or market executive is essentially alien to Catholic tradition and practice.

Recent research suggests that what has characterised the best examples of Catholic school leadership in the past is (i) the practice of servant—leadership and (ii) the spiritual capital resources of headteachers to be effective faith leaders.[22]

Punnachet argues that as Catholics have the greatest model of servant-leadership in the person of Jesus Christ, this should provide the model for Catholic school leadership at its best.

My own research[23] has demonstrated the value of school leaders who possess spiritual capital, defined as:

> resources of faith and values derived from commitment to a religious tradition, and possessed by persons who do not act simply as professionals but as professionals and witnesses.[24]

The challenge in a globalised world that wants to make school leaders into corporate leaders is to hold fast to our distinctive concept of Catholic Servant leadership as a vocational and humane expression of Christian leadership in education.

The distinctive nature of faith school leadership at the level of Headship involves, at its best, the demonstration of high levels of secular professional vision and competences, allied to a high level of personal commitment and witness to the religious, spiritual and social practices of the faith mission of the school.

A Catholic school self-evaluation exercise will involve an attempt to assess the reality of this, as expressed not only by the headteacher but also by the governors and senior teachers who represent the leadership matrix of the school.

e. An Educational Culture and Ethos of 'Vocation' and 'Formation' (VCF criteria)

The contemporary secular education world internationally is dominated by the discourse of 'training'—the training of skills and competences in young people; the training of teachers; training for school leadership and so on. Training as an educational and social process is, of course, important for young people and for adults but training is only a sub-set of a larger and more holistic educational concept which Catholic have rightly called 'formation'.

Catholic educational discourse and practice should be based upon our religious culture and heritage and it is a discourse and practice of the formation of persons, educationally, spiritually, religiously, morally and socially. This is the Catholic holistic and comprehensive concept of an education.

The contemporary challenge for all schools is not to reduce this total experience to the mere resourcing of persons with a set of trained skills.

In a similar way, Catholic schools have to resist a dominant cultural notion that the whole purpose of a 'good' education is to obtain a 'good' job. Of course, everyone needs and deserves a good job and educators have a responsibility to help them to that goal—this is the realisation of the Parable of the Talents. However, as Christopher Jamison, OSB has argued, if we follow the charism of Cardinal Newman that,' God has created me to do him some definite service', then the concept of a vocation should be 'at the heart of the Catholic curriculum'.[25] The challenge is, in a universal culture of jobs, for Catholic schools to keep alive the culture of vocations (in all its different forms)[26] with its essential correlate of service to others.

Conclusion: Is Catholic School Self-Evaluation Possible?

Given the increasing power and influence of *Performative Secular Evaluation* of schools across the world, it may seem totally unrealistic to ask Catholic schools to take on the additional challenges of Mission Catholic Evaluation. However, a failure to engage seriously with the requirements of *MCEV* will, in the long term lead to Mission Drift and the gradual cultural and educational incorporation of Catholic schools into State mandated educational regimes.

Notes

1. M. Potterton & C. Northmore, 'Improving Schools Through Evaluation: the experience of Catholic schools in South Africa'. In: *International Studies in Catholic Education,* Vol. 6/No.2 (2014), 178–190. Dr Mark Potterton is the Principal of Holy Family School, Parktown, South Africa and Colin Northmore is the Headmaster of Sacred Heart College, Johannesburg.

2. *Ibid.,* 189.

3. *Ibid.,*: Potterton and Northmore note that 'our evaluations in Catholic schools look closely at the religious ethos of the schools' (185) and comment on the value of a document provided by Religious Congregations ('school proprietors') entitled, 'Signs of God's Presence' for evaluating religious ethos, 189.

4. G. Grace & L. O'Keefe (eds) *International Handbook of Catholic Education* 2 Volumes (Dordrecht: Springer, 2007).

5. 'National competitiveness has increasingly become a central preoccupation of governance strategies throughout the world'. Quoted in S. Ball, *Education Plc* (London: Routledge, 2007), 7.

6. In research studies conducted in 1995 and in 2002; I noted that many headteachers were extensively using the language and concepts of external inspection regimes in discussing educational issues. A form of linguistic colonisation was in progress. See G. Grace, *School Leadership: Beyond Education Management* (London: Falmer Press, 1995) and G. Grace, *Catholic Schools: Mission, Markets and Morality* (London: Routledge Falmer, 2002a).

7. See: Potterton & Northmore, 'Improving Schools Through Evaluation', 2014.

[8] The labelling of these two modes of evaluation is designed to show what is the dominant perspective in each case. Thus, Performativity is dominant in Performative Secular Evaluation (PSEV), while Mission is dominant (or should be) in Mission Catholic Evaluation (MCEV).

[9] This criterion has been influenced by the description used by Potterton and Northmore (2014) 'Improving Schools Through Evaluation', 186, in reporting that 'Catholic ethos was practised vibrantly' at Loreto School, Pretoria.

[10] Congregation for Catholic Education, *The Catholic School* (1977), 34.

[11] *Ibid.*, 36.

[12] As one example, the Catholic Bishops of England and Wales have insisted that secondary schools should ring-fence 10% of timetabled time for Religious Education. This was known to many of the headteachers with whom I conducted research interviews in the late 1990s. Some of them 'confessed' that arising from the pressures of PSEV, extra time had been allocated to English, Maths and Science at the expense of RE.

[13] See C. Jamison OSB (2013) 'God has created me to do him some definite service' (Newman): vocation at the heart of the Catholic curriculum'. In: *International Studies in Catholic Education*, Vol. 5/No. 1 (2013), 10–22, for proposals about how this could be done.

[14] Congregation for Catholic Education, *The Catholic School*, 85.

[15] *Ibid.*, 2.

[16] A. Wright, *Spiritual Pedagogy* (Abingdon: Culham College Institute, 1998) 24, contrasts anthropological approaches to spirituality 'understood as that area of human awareness, experience and inner feeling that illuminated the purpose and meaning of life', with theological approaches which relate all of this to an awareness of the presence of God.

[17] For a more detailed discussion see G. Grace 'Mission Integrity: Contemporary Challenges for Catholic School Leaders'. In: K. Leithwood & P. Hallinger (eds) *Second International Handbook of Educational Leadership and Administration* (Dordrecht: Kluwer Academic Publishers, 2002b), 427–449.

[18] Catholic Bishops Conference of England & Wales, *The Common Good in Education* (London: Catholic Education Service, 1997), 10.

[19] See D. Harvey, *A Brief History of Neoliberalism* (Oxford: Oxford University Press, 2005) 2: 'Neoliberalism is a theory of political economic practices that proposes that human well-being can best be advanced by liberating individual entrepreneurial freedoms and skills within an institutional framework of free markets... if markets do not exist in areas such as education, health care, social security, then they must be created by state action if necessary'.

[20] Catholic Bishops Conference of England and Wales, *The Common Good in Education*, 16.

[21] S. Ball, *Education Plc* (London: Routledge, 2007).

[22] See T. Punnachet, 'Catholic servant-leadership: going beyond the secular paradigm'. In: *International Studies in Catholic Education*, Vol. 1/No. 2 (2009), 117–134 and G. Grace, 'Renewing Spiritual Capital: an urgent priority for the future of Catholic Education'. In: *International Studies in Catholic Education*, Vol. 2/No. 2 (2010), 117–128.

[23] Grace, *Catholic Schools*.

[24] *Ibid.*, 2002a, Chapter 10. This composite definition is derived from the conclusion of this book and also from a later article elaborating the nature of spiritual capital: see Grace 'Renewing Spiritual Capital'.

[25] C. Jamison, 'God has created me to do him some definite service' (Newman) (2013), 10.

[26] The culture of vocations has been historically associated with vocations for the priesthood and the religious life. Post-Vatican II concepts of lay vocations now have greater salience with emphasis upon the lay vocations of parenthood, volunteer international service and public service occupations of various types.

Contemporary Catholic Headship and the Pursuit of Authenticity in Justice

Dr Simon Uttley

Dr Simon Uttley is a serving Headteacher in a Catholic High School in the South of England. He is also Professor and Course Director of 'Catholic Education and the Common Good' at the London programme of the University of Notre Dame, U.S.A. as well as Visiting Lecturer at University College London, Institute of Education and St Mary's University, London.

The Contemporary Catholic Headteacher: Caught in or Sustained by the Web of Tradition and Practice?

> Two roads diverged in a yellow wood
> And sorry I could not travel both
> And be one traveller, long I stood
> And looked down one as far as I could
> To where it bent in the undergrowth.[1]

ROST'S WELL-KNOWN, IF often misunderstood poem considers choices and what economists call the 'opportunity cost', or lost opportunity of choices not taken.

But as the second and third stanzas make clear, the poem is very much concerned with how the varying paths will look *in retrospect* as, in embarking on one path, the sacrifice is made. It cannot be undone, though it can be regretted at leisure.

> And both that morning equally lay
> In leaves no step had trodden black.[2]

Humans are past masters at retrospect: indeed, we have made from it both an academic discipline—*history*—as well as a source of cultural capital—*tradition*. Though some might see tradition as a form of romanticised coercion—the past illegitimately trespassing into the future—perhaps to protect vested interests, nevertheless Catholics, including *this* Catholic Headteacher of an English, inner city Catholic secondary school, are locked into a complex blend of traditions. The *apostolic tradition* charts the truth claims transmitted through an unbroken chain of bishops in whose dioceses, and with canonical approval, we ply our trade as Catholic school leaders, as spiritual leaders, as role models. As such leaders we have what the later Wittgenstein would have called our own *language game*[3] which, at first glance, is identical to so many other non-denominational schools as to risk imploding into kitsch. The 'Pursuit of Excellence', 'No Child Left Behind' or the intellectually suspect, if well intended, 'Every Child Succeeds'. More 'Catholic' is 'Uniqueness of the Individual', or, perhaps, something about vocations. Such warm words, as comfortable as a pair of favourite slippers, seep into our language such that they cease to be words but, instead, morph into signs, pointing us—the students, parents, Governors—towards the sunlit uplands of educational nirvana and, understandably contribute to the perception that the Catholic school is somehow defined not in terms of the following of the crucified and risen Christ but, instead, by 'being caring' and 'having good discipline'. As Saussure said, 'nearly all institutions ... are based on signs'[4] and that job-lot of crucifixes that reside at the back of the R.E. room, or perhaps the Chapel, reflects that the Catholic Church and its schools are no exception.

For some of our schools we trumpet—sometimes literally—our 'traditions' from the galleries in the form of our distinctive liturgies. Be it *Shine Jesus Shine!* or Baroque motet, our liturgy, like a sacrament, is an outward sign of the (hoped for) inner grace of our schools. It is probably why we like to invite mum, dad, grandma and granddad to the carol service, the Patronal Feast Day or that particularly moving Easter liturgy. Oh, and if it is done well it does not half help with the marketing of the school too!

For some of us of a certain age—or from a dwindling number of (predominantly independent) Catholic schools where the phenomena can still be found, we may recall those 'professional religious'[5]—those women and men, habited or not, who walked our lofty corridors and, for good or ill, very literally enfleshed the tradition. We only have to recall how stories of 'a convent education' have crossed the Rubicon from our Catholic, minority sub-culture to enter the wider public consciousness as a byword for—taking its most positive hermeneutic—*rigour and excellence*.

But, of course, our traditions subsist within broader, national narratives. Narratives, which remind us of the extent to which, as maintained Catholic schools at least, we owe our existence to the benevolence—or pragmatism—of the State. The Catholic maintained school essentially finds itself under benign, somewhat comfortable 'house arrest'; not dissimilar to that experienced by our well-heeled recusant forbears who, with the resources to pay off the post-Reformation state, could keep a chaplain, say their prayers and do *their* thing as long as it did not trespass into the dominant hegemony of the establishment politics of the day.

Structurally, too, our schools sit comfortably within the paradigm preferred by the State.[6] For a start, there is the traditional (essentially Victorian) conception of what constitutes 'school'. This includes, *inter alia*, the social benefit of housing and socialising the (sometimes rather challenging) *youth* for a time, which arguably, dates from the passing of the Forster Act in 1870. And since that time all our schools—Catholic Protestant, non-denominational—have essentially included the same ingredients: organised play areas, classrooms and timetables for dividing and enframing education, a space for collective moral instruction (assembly hall), age stratification, and an ethos of discipline and self-management.[7] In socialising the young we, understandably, teach them to conform and keep them under close observation, just as the Headteacher herself is surveilled. The French existentialist, Michel Foucault wrote compellingly about the surveilled society, including references to prisons whose architecture was such as to allow all the inmates to be viewed at all times—the so-called panopticon.[8] And such 'accountability' takes its toll on recruiting new school leaders. Five years ago I would speak to Deputy Headteachers who would ask 'How do I become a Head or Principal?' In the last three years as many have ventured another question; a question which excoriates the very façade of a smooth, linear 'progression' to Headship: 'remind me again ...' they ask, 'why do I need the pressure?'

But we, as adults can at least make a choice: but what of the effect of the data-driven panopticon on the young? As Headteachers, we may or may not choose to have CCTV on every corner of our buildings, but, as folk who can so easily spend as much time trying to *keep* our job ('Are we Ofsted-ready?') as actually *doing* our job, we will, undoubtedly, be very good at 'tracking and monitoring'. With benign intent, we bury the *divinely created, uniquely called child of God* beneath levels, target grades, gendered, socio-economic and ethnically enframed tagging and all those myriad of 'lenses' which, like the fairground hall of mirrors, can surely distort.

The Catholic Headteacher and the Danger of Education-as-Qualification?

The distorting effect of data-driven panopticism may well take the form of excessive genuflection to the spread sheet[9], but, more significantly surely is the effect on children.[10] Could our *high performing, pastorally caring* Catholic schools, as obedient vehicles of the State, run the risk of being complicit in distorting the young person into ever-greater self-criticism? Could this lead to them believing that, just as their *qualifications* (a word whose etymology rests on the dialectic of being 'entitled to' and 'restricted from') is externally benchmarked from their earliest schooling, their self-worth, too, is somehow *outside* of themselves and not of their own? In a culture where we can be 'Friended' and 'Unfriended', 'Followed' and 'Unfollowed' at the tap of a smartphone, such a *dis-location*, a kind of emotional version of Cartesian dualism, is no mere theoretical abstraction.

In 2009 Whelan noted that 'England has implemented more of the policies that would be expected to improve performance in a school system than any other country in the world'.[11] Yet, the UK educational well-being indicator in 2013 was below average and below Latvia, Slovakia and Lithuania.[12]

A 2015 international comparative study of children's subjective well-being in 15 countries, ranked England 14th out of 15 for satisfaction with life as a whole.[13] England was in the bottom half of the table (that is ranking 9 or lower out of 15) for 24 out of 30 aspects of life, with especially low rankings for children's satisfaction with their 'self' and with their school lives. With 2142 Catholic schools in England in 2015—10% of the estate of schools[14]—charged with 'delivering' an education which, at the aggregate level at least, appears flawed, means that we too are surely part of the problem.

The Catholic School Leader and the 'Qualification' of School Admissions

So far it has been suggested how, through the panopticon of data, the success or otherwise of the entirety of students seven years of secondary education is, to a large extent, back-read from performance largely measured on terminal examinations, themselves predicated on education being for 'skills acquisition' and 'employability'. Equally, the 'Catholicity' or otherwise of our students can, in some of our schools at least, also be 'back-read', for example by setting admissions criteria which ultimately centre on the child's parents willingness—or savviness—to get them to Mass. They 'practice' if their parents take them; they are 'lapsed' if their parents do not take them. This can then be self-fulfilling as successive generations of children, deemed 'un-churched'—

and disproportionately represented in the less well off—then also 'fail' to take their own children to Mass, directly affecting their children's opportunities to benefit from a Catholic school. While there are no easy answers to this phenomenon, surely a recurring theme for the contemporary Headteacher, it surely must remain a problem for us in the sense that it should provoke a sense of uneasiness. As Catholic schools we place the poor—the less articulate—at the heart of our mission.[15] Or do we? To employ the language of another French philosopher, Jacques Derrida, we have, in our admissions codes, a wonderful example of 'restricted hospitality'—of a warm welcome, 'on condition'; a commitment to inclusion 'on our terms'.[16] While it may seem somewhat 'evangelical' for Catholic taste to employ the oft-manipulated rhetorical device 'what would Jesus do', it is surely instructive to ask what the Galilean carpenter's son might think of a school, built in his name, employing expensive lawyers to keep out 'non-qualifying' children.

The Catholic Headteacher—and Student—Caught Up in a World of Master Narratives and Punch and Judy Binaries.

When narratives become embedded, they may become what Lyotard called 'metanarratives'[17] almost standing outside of individual consciousness, yet constantly informing collective consciousness. Democracy and the rule of law are two such metanarratives particularly promoted by the UK Government in its contemporary commitment to 'promote British values'.[18] Guidance and the eponymous 'toolkits' are produced to help schools 'promote' such metanarratives as a counterbalance to extremism, also creating space for critics of Church schools to suggest that 'them Catholics' (note the *othering* again) themselves promote fundamentalism in being faith-based in the first place. If only we were all like those nice 'secular' schools, tolerance would pour forth like a raging river and our children would be free at last from the shackles of oppressive, mediaeval, *Romish* metaphysics.

Sadly—or happily depending on one's point of view—this particular narrative is a busted flush. The so-called 'Trojan Horse' cases[19], where it was suggested that the Governing Bodies of a number of Birmingham schools had given into Islamic extremism, is a case in hand. Not one of those schools was a faith-based school, though our 'quality' press lost no time in morphing the story into a discussion on 'faith schools' (*The Guardian*), the expression itself—*faith school*—suggesting an almost theocratic menace.

The narrative binary of *'religion'* on one side and *'tolerance and progress'* on the other—that could be called, after the famous warring puppets a *Punch and Judy binary*—represents, a baseless attempt to render a group—in this case schools with a religious character—*other*. Almost 'not English/British'. *Othering* in this way is a device much loved by politicians who always enjoy the *Punch and Judy* binary as it brings people 'onside'. (It is noteworthy that the U.S. pursuit of communists and other subversives in the mid twentieth century was badged not as the pursuit of extremism but rather as the House of *Un-American Activities* Committee). And some of our famous saints in Reformation times were not sentenced to death for saying Mass or for *being* Catholic but for 'treason' (Simpson, 2010).[20] That tolerance lies at the heart of our faith in the absolute hospitality of the person of Jesus is easily forgotten in a world of 'fast-food' reportage, as thirsty for 'bogey men' and easy answers—as it ever has.

But our English and Welsh Church, too, is not immune from narratives. In addition to those narratives we celebrate—liturgy, doctrine, revelation—we also have our English Catholic history which, as with all history, represents an act of retrospective compromise. Why a compromise?

Firstly, as humans we try and impose retrospective meaning where it may not exist, a process we call *making sense* of things. Secondly, to the extent that we only ever hear the voices that had their say—so often the 'entitled' voices of the day—this, too, leads to the preservation and promotion of a corpus of material which is inevitably compromised in its provenance.

Since the sixteenth century, in England, the core metanarratives of Catholic Church and State have diverged radically: explosively in the Protestant Reformation, yet very much in evidence in the Victorian period where, in its *'othering'* of 'Roman' Catholics, the mistrust and hostility was accentuated by the racial discrimination of the Irish poor.[21] There was much understandable pomp and meaning-making associated with the Restoration of the Hierarchy and the centrality of education was not lost on Cardinal Wiseman:

> The Catholic church is springing up again, ... 'It had left its tap root' ... Under the religious soil of England, from which new suckers are now shooting upwards; the sap which was believed to be drained out is rising in them once more. The old plant senses again the waters, and revives, endowed with a marvellous versatility.

He went on 'our weak side is the education of our children'...'whom our poverty prevents us from bringing up as we would desire'.[22] Yet, at the same time, the shape of Catholic education that developed was by no means straightforward. 'Influencers'—on the Church and subsequently its education missions included the (presence of the) Irish poor, the old Catholic gentry, the Catholic middle class, the clergy, Pope Pius IX but also the pragmatism of the State. But the 'foreignness' of Catholicism— even to the point of the State actively legislating against the Catholic Church—can never be forgotten as epitomised by the hostility shown when the Church wished to appoint Bishops once more. The Ecclesiastical Titles Act 1851 was blatantly anti-Catholic, making it a criminal offence for anyone outside the Church of England to use any episcopal title of any city, town or place, or of any territory or district (under any designation or description whatsoever), in the United Kingdom. Incited by anti-Catholic elements and, indeed, Russell as Prime Minister of the day, serious anti-Catholic riots took place in November 1850 in Liverpool and other cities. Nearly 900,000 Protestants petitioned the Queen to stop what they called 'papal aggression' and Guy Fawkes Day, 1850, saw numerous symbolic denunciations, and a handful of cases of violence.[23] The significance of this to the contemporary Catholic Headteacher may seem vague, but what it exemplifies is, once again, the willingness and ability of the State to *other* a community—including its children—within a system which trumpets 'democracy and the rule of law'. As every teacher knows, if a child is constantly in fear, made to feel 'other', made to feel she should be grateful for what she is offered and that her freedom is only ever on the terms of another—one who holds power—then an inevitable consequence is the infantilising of the child; a perpetual juvenility. Taking that child to mean the Victorian English Catholic Church it is at least plausible to see such forced juvenility as an element in what was to become a master-client relationship between the State and the Church's education function. We are so eager to please.

The Catholic Headteacher as 'Righteous Subversive'

We live in interesting times. 'Fundamental British Values' (Department for Education, 2014) suggests a new *metaphysics* of what is nationally acceptable; metaphysical in the sense of being abstract and difficult to pin down. The 'Prevent Strategy'[24] ensures our school IT systems are kitted out with the appropriate technology to stop even our five year olds from being radicalised and commentators such as Polly Toynbee can assert that schools with a religious character represent 'a state sponsored way for churches to fill their empty pews with anxious new parents kneeling to gods they don't believe in'.[25] Hardly the climate to advocate subversion. Yet what 'our' (assuming an homogeneous group) Catholic history reminds *this* Catholic Headteacher is this: as Catholic educators we *are* 'different'; we *are* 'other'. If not we cease to understand our identity. Anecdotally, we tend to be at our best when we are under pressure (we are a minority with several centuries experience of persecution) and if it feels too comfortable we are probably doing something wrong. So the very last thing we should be surprised about is that what we do can be controversial. (Did not someone once say, 'blessed are you when people reproach you, and persecute you and speaking falsely, say all manner of evil against you, for my sake'). So, let's try and make Saints out of Year 10.

The Catholic Headteacher: Subverting the Sterile Narrative of What Constitutes Achievement by Keeping Children 'Busy in the Vineyard'

Catholic schools surely must present children—of all ages—with as many experiences of the possibility to do justice and, in so doing, let them know they matter. That they have power; agency. Let's help them move from the theory of good and evil to the practice of virtue by filling our teaching, pastoral life and liturgies with that which the young are so instinctively attuned but which we do so much to deaden in our compartmentalised, sanitised curricula. The pursuit of justice. Finding the moral, and celebrating the affective, in all things.

The opportunity to help a sick or disabled person, perhaps on a school pilgrimage to Lourdes, has long been a wonderful 'extra' for those who can afford the time and money. But this is to completely undervalue it. It is the chance to experience justice/injustice: Why has this happened to this person; what can I do to help and what does it mean to me to know I can make a difference? It means I matter. Or the Fair Trade project, or supporting campaigns such as *Send My Friend to School* (which aims to help the thirty seven million children who cannot go to school) draw children into the possibility of justice and to be moved by what they experience. And in our culture which routinely underappreciates the elderly to the point of scandal, encountering the elderly too is an opportunity for children and young people to feel they matter, feel they have power to do good and learn from others. The work at a Food Bank, a sadly well-understood initiative in the United Kingdom at the time of writing, brings students face to face with the aporia—the impasse—of, on one side the metanarrative of 'constant progress as a wealthy first world country' and on the other the absolute absence of such wealth in the lives of the poor.

But further still, the curriculum needs to break down its walls of arbitrary specialisms and bring together deep reflection, the moral questions alive in all academic discourse and stir children's souls. As every teacher knows, *if it matters to them, and they matter to you* their learning will be transformed. This is not preachy or 'left wing',—one way, indeed, would be to draw on the approach of qualifications such as the International Baccalaureate, still the preserve of a niche of (predominantly independent) schools. Let us not continue, on the one hand, to teach R.E., while allowing a sclerotic, Victorian school system to extinguish the real secret to learning—and to a life worth living—*mattering*. Let us welcome the moment when *educare* is transfigured to *educere*[26], when education-as-moulding becomes education as a 'leading out'; as epiphany?

Notes

[1]   R. Frost, *The Road Not Taken and Other Selected Poems* (Radford, VA: Wilder Publications, 2011).

[2]   *Ibid.*

[3]   L. Wittgenstein, *Philosophical Investigations*, P. Michael, ed. & G. A. Elisabeth, trans., (Oxford: Wiley Blackwell, 2009).

[4]   F. Saussure, *Saussure's Third Course of Lectures on General Linguistics: 1910–1911* R. Harris and E. A. Komatsu, eds., & E. A. Komatsu, trans., (Oxford: Pergamon Press, 1993).

[5]   J. Lydon, 'Transmission of the Charism: a major challenge for Catholic education'. In: *International Studies in Catholic Education* Vol. 1/No. 1 (2009), 42–58; 51.

[6]   P. G. Hoffman *et al.*, (R. English, ed. and intro.) *The Essentials of Freedom: The Odea and Practice of Ordered Liberty in the Twentieth Century as explored at Kenyon College*, Conference Proceedings (Gambier, Ohio, 1960).

7   K. Flint, & N. Peim, *Rethinking the Education Improvement Agenda: a critical philosophical approach* (London: Continuum, 2012).

8   M. Foucault, *Discipline and Punish: the birth of a prison* A. Lane, trans. (London: Penguin Books, 1977).

9   In its current (2015) form, the 'holy of holies' being 'Raiseonline', the Ofsted-based national data vehicle by which school—and school leader—'performance' is substantially judged.

10   See: J. Arthur, *The Ebbing Tide* (Leominster: Gracewing, 1995).

11   F. Whelan, *Lessons Learned: how good policies produce better schools* (London: Fenton Whelan, 2009).

12   UNICEF, *Child Well-Being in Rich Countries: a comparative overview* (Florence: UNICEF, 2013).

13   The Children's Society, *The Good Childhood Report* (London: The Children's Society, 2015).

14   Catholic Education Service of England and Wales *Infographic.*, 2015 (Retrieved Jan 8, 2016) http://www.catholiceducation.org.uk/news/ces-news/item/1003019-2015-census-infographic.

15   G. Grace, *Catholic Schools: Mission, Markets and Morality* (London: Routledge Falmer, 2002).

16   J. Derrida, *Of Hospitality, Anne Dufourmantelle invites Jacques Derrida to respond* (Stanford: Stanford University Press, 2000). See E. Lévinas, *Totality and Infinity* (Pittsburgh: Duquesne University Press, 1969).

17   J.-F. Lyotard, *The Post-Modern Condition: a report on knowledge* (Minneapolis: University of Minnesota Press, 1984).

18   Department for Education, *Promoting Fundamental British Values as Part of SMSC in Schools* (London: Department for Education, 2014).

19   J. Romain, 'The Trojan horse affair has been a wake-up call on faith schools', *The Guardian*, 30 October 2014.

20   R. Simpson, *Edmund Campion*, revised, edited and enlarged by Fr Peter Joseph (Leominster: Gracewing/Freedom Press, 2010; 1867).

21   D. Paz, *Popular Anti-Catholicism in Mid-Victorian England* (Stanford: Stanford University Press, 1992). The 'enemy at the gate' continues to animate the British sensibilities to this day, immigration being the second most significant issue for voters in the 2015 General Election after the economy (Ipsos-Mori, 2015) and a continued ambivalence towards the extent of welcome to be given to refugees.

22   N. Wiseman, 'The Religious and Social Position of Catholics in England: an address delivered to the Catholic Congress of Malines', 21 August 1863 (Dublin: James Duffy), 16.

23   K. Theodore Hoppen, *The Mid-Victorian Generation, 1846–1886* (Oxford: Oxford University Press, 2000).

24 Home Office, *Prevent Strategy* (London: Home Office, 2011).

25 P. Toynbee *Our Supporters*, Accord Coalition, 2015: http://accordcoalition.org.uk/our-supporters/ (retrieved 5 January 2016).

26 M. Craft, 'Education for Diversity'. In: M. Craft (ed.), *Education and Cultural Pluralism* (London & Philadelphia: Falmer Press, 1984), 5–26.

12 TRUSTEESHIP AND THE GOVERNANCE OF CATHOLIC SCHOOLS

Dr Christopher Storr

Christopher Storr is a Research Associate at both University College London Institute of Education and St Mary's University Twickenham. This chapter argues that many governors seem unaware of the Catholic Church's insistence that education in its schools must have a distinct character: one that makes them qualitatively different from all other schools. In consequence, the schools' inherited spiritual capital is being eroded. Trustees need to make greater efforts to ensure governors are fully aware of the resources already available to them if their schools are to remain true to the principles on which they have been founded.

THE DIVISIONAL EDUCATION officer was on the phone. A man not known for having much of an opinion about the county education office, he was in full flow that summer afternoon in the early 1960s. Something had gone wrong with the delivery of a mobile classroom to a primary school in his patch, and he held me responsible. But I did not care much. I certainly cared that the promised mobile had apparently disappeared en route for the school, but of the school managers' views I cared not a jot. No one cared about managers and governors at the county office in those days except, perhaps, for the governing body of the voluntary aided grammar school where the county education officer was a governor.

Such an incident seems impossible today, so great has been the revolution in the power and influence of governing bodies since the 1980 legislation, which, inter alia, abolished primary school managers and replaced them with governors[1].

Trustees are dioceses and certain religious orders. They are the *éminences grises* behind Catholic schools. They establish the schools in the first place, own the sites of the buildings and the buildings themselves, and appoint the foundation governors. That is about the extent of their formal powers.

Diocesan trustees delegate day-to-day oversight of their schools to a clerical or lay official—the schools' commissioner or director of schools. The system appears to work smoothly. There have been few disputes of note, and these seem to be a London phenomenon, involving the Archdioceses of Southwark and Westminster. They concerned matters to do with the admission of pupils and the appointment of teachers.

Before 1980, it had been easy for Catholic school trustees to control what went on in their schools. The managing body of a primary school comprised just six members: four foundation managers appointed by the trustees, two appointed by the local authorities. It was therefore not difficult to find loyal parishioners to perform such managerial duties as came their way. Moreover, there was no limit on the number of managerships or governorships a person could hold. It was quite possible (and did happen) for a priest who wanted to make his mark in the education field to be a manager or governor of a dozen or more schools.

This did not matter much. In my early days in Southwark an incident arose in a primary school relating to the new admissions arrangements introduced by the 1980 Act. On enquiry, it transpired that the managing/governing body had not met for seven years. The parish priest had managed the school on his own without bothering anybody. No one had noticed.

It is not possible in a short chapter to detail the many changes that have taken place in the powers of governing bodies over the last 35 years. One related feature must, however, be noted. Whilst the size of governing bodies has increased substantially, and made the task of trustees finding foundation governors very onerous, the foundation's majority has almost been eliminated. With the arrival of elected teacher and parent governors, and ever tighter restrictions on the number of governorships an individual might hold, the certainty that trustees formerly had that their wishes would prevail in running their schools no longer exists. If they want to exercise any influence in a wide range of issues, this can be achieved only by persuasion.

Whilst all this has been going on, changes have been taking place in the nature of the schools themselves.

First, there is a contradictory change in the school rolls. CES statistics show that overall numbers of pupils, including baptised Catholics, continue to increase year by year. But the increase in the numbers of non-Catholics is greater so the percentage of Catholic pupils is in steady decline: from 75% in 2008 to 71% in 2012.[2]

Second, at the same time, the same statistics show an ever growing number of non-Catholic teachers in the schools: 58% in 2008 to 55% in 2012. For many years, indeed, less than 50% of teachers in Catholic secondary schools have been Catholic.

In summary, therefore, we have ever-increasingly empowered governing bodies responsible for schools that employ growing numbers of non-Catholic teachers to teach a declining percentage of Catholic pupils.

Does This Matter?

Grace, in his pioneering work, concluded that it does.[3] He interviewed 60 Catholic headteachers from urban areas and discussed with them the tensions between academic success and market values, as increasingly strongly promulgated by the state, and the mission integrity of Catholic schools as manifest in their spiritual, moral and social justice commitments. He concluded that one essential element in the fabric of Catholic schools was spiritual capital, which he defined as resources of faith and values derived from commitment to a religious tradition. This, he argued, was what had provided the dynamic drive of their mission in the past and helped them preserve their mission integrity in the present. He found that this resource was not being renewed, and that, in consequence, there was a real danger of its being eroded by the constant demands of a state driven by an overarching conviction that the only valid yardstick by which schools might be assessed was that of market forces.

Grace acknowledged that there are other players in this field. One of these is clearly governing bodies. In the light of the key position governors now occupy in the lives of their schools, I decided to develop Grace's work by examining the extent to which they were aware of these tensions, and, if they were, how they were seeking to hold the ring, as it were, between the two positions. It was also essential to look at primary schools as well as secondary, and those in a variety of communities other than inner city: urban, suburban, and, if possible, rural.

No one involved in education at this time will need to be reminded of the torrent of requirements and 'advice' pouring from both the Department for Education (DfE) and Ofsted.[4] The overriding conviction in this Brave New World is that schools must at all costs serve the nation by producing efficient producers of wealth so that the country will continue to grow, presumably in perpetuity. It remains to be seen if the recent work of the French economist Thomas Piketty comes to exercise any moderating influence.[5]

To facilitate this, a culture of competition has been fostered, with schools graded at this level and that, so that all may see at a glance which are claimed to be succeeding and which failing. Woe betide the board of governors of a school that is found not to be up to the mark!

It can be so easily overlooked that the Catholic Church has its own view about the nature and purpose of education, and that this began to be articulated a decade before the state began to get round to it in a more haphazard way. Needless to say, the Church's vision could scarcely be further removed from that of the state. Starting in 1977, four seminal documents had been published by the Vatican by the end of the century.[6]

In very brief summary, what emerges from these, is that 'Christ is the foundation of the whole educational enterprise'[7] and it is this single basic fact that makes the Catholic school different. Its task is to provide 'a synthesis of faith and culture and a synthesis of faith and life'.[8] The educative process is not simply 'the attainment of knowledge, but the acquisition of values and the discovery of truth'.[9] Young people have to be taught to share their personal lives with God and '[t]hey are to overcome their individualism and discover ... their specific vocation to live responsibly in a community with others and to serve God in their brethren and to make the world a better place'.[10] All knowledge comes from God and teachers must seek out the religious resonances in all subjects, geography, history, literature, physical education and the sciences and so on.

The 1998 Vatican document on education notes 'a tendency to reduce education to its purely technical and practical aspects' rather than to 'foster values and vision' and to forget that 'education always presupposes and involves a definition of man and life'.[11] Catholic Schools must promote a Christian vision of the world, of life, of culture and of history ... 'a set of values to be acquired and truths to be discovered'.[12]

Local bishops' conferences were urged to carry this work forward within their local contexts, and the bishops of England and Wales and the Catholic Education Service were not slow to take up the challenge with a series of documents that were increasingly critical of government policy.[13]

> The National Curriculum is not an end in itself. All this contributes to our understanding of the way God works in our lives and thus of our understanding of and response to Him... The way in which we and our pupils work is then seen as contributing to God's creation and continuing purpose.[14]

> There appears to be increasing confusion in society about the nature and purpose of education, stemming from the tendency to judge the success of both individuals and of society as a whole by economic criteria ... However, economic self-interest should not be the basis of ... a commitment [to education]. Education is, primarily about 'human flourishing' ... and the development of the whole

person ... Catholic social teaching has constantly been aware of the tendency of free market economic theory to claim more of itself than is warranted. In particular, an economic creed that insists the greater good of society is best served by each individual pursuing his or her own self-interest is likely to find itself encouraging individual selfishness ... Christian teaching that service of others is of greater value than service to self is sure to seem at odds with the ethos of a capitalist economy ... Education is not a commodity offered for sale ... Teachers and their pupils are not economic units whose value is seen merely as a cost element on the school's balance sheet ... Education is a service provided by society for the benefit of all its young people, in particular for the benefit of the most vulnerable and the most disadvantaged—those whom we have a sacred duty to serve ...The desire to 'succeed' at all costs has encouraged some schools and colleges to discriminate in their selection procedures against pupils with special educational needs or from disadvantaged families ... Others are permanently excluding pupils with emotional needs or from disadvantaged families ... In some schools, the most able and experienced staff are deployed to teach the most able pupils ...The less able may not be permitted to enter public examinations ... specialist resources ... are sometimes made available to the more able students.[15]

So there, in Brief, is the Dichotomy

Are governors aware of it, and if so, how are they seeking to resolve the tensions between the two rival philosophies? Is their school identifiable as a 'Blackpool rock' institution, where the Catholic ethos runs right through it, or is it the 'dual function' school first defined as such by McLaughlin in 1990—a school largely indistinguishable from any other, but with a bit of denominational RE bolted on the end?[16]

One of the first surprises I had when I began my work was that the relationship between governors and their bishop and diocese are in general tenuous. Few of those I surveyed thought there had been a commissioning service at the beginning of their term of office—at its most basic an occasion when the bishop meets and welcomes governors to their role in participating in the mission of the Church, and outlines the particular opportunities and responsibilities they have. It seems a pity that such an obvious opportunity to start the enterprise off on the right foot is missed and that so many think of their bishop as 'shadowy and remote'. One chairman said, with a laugh, 'I do not think he knows who I am', whilst another described the hurdles she had to jump to get the bishop to visit her school for the very first time in almost 30 years.

The situation is exacerbated when links with the diocese and the schools' commission are examined. If there is a priest or religious on the governing body, he or she is expected to look after this area of work 'because it's their thing' as one governor put it. The only time the governing body generally gets involved with the diocese is either when something has gone badly wrong, for example, an adverse Ofsted report, or there is a need to appoint a new head teacher (and sometimes a deputy).

In respect of curriculum matters, the Church, as has already been noted, has a clearly expressed view. How many governors are aware of this? They also have a duty to meet the needs of the National Curriculum, and other policies from the secular authorities that may not sit easily with the teachings of the Church. When I carried out my research[17], more than half the governors told me their schools had adopted all or most of their LA's curriculum policy without modification.[18] Now that so many schools have become academies, where are governors finding informed guidance on this crucial issue? Several have appointed non-diocesan advisers, but it is unclear how many have any knowledge of the Catholic dimension. Some skilled and experienced Catholic educationists advertise support services on the web, but not nearly enough, it seems, to cater for the need. Diocesan websites do not suggest anything like sufficient activity in this crucially important field. So how much of what is taught is based on 'a specific concept of the world, of man, and of history'? What the evidence seems to be suggesting is, again, that McLaughlin's 'dual function school' is alive and well.

There is a widely held view that, for Catholics, none of this matters at all. The essential defining feature of a Catholic school is its ethos, and Catholics know a Catholic ethos when they find it. But what is it, and do governors monitor it to ensure that all is well? Since the Vatican and a number of distinguished scholars have different takes on this, it is hardly surprising that governors do, too. Thus, in some schools it is based on the externals: pictures of the pope or the bishop, crucifixes in corridors and classrooms; in others it is to do with relationships; the involvement of parish clergy; and nurturing pupils in their faith and the provision of prayer rooms. But in others, there is nothing specifically Catholic: 'it's a caring environment;' or 'you can just tell it's a Catholic school'. And what is to be made of these? 'the way the children [behave] reflects the caring love of neighbour ethos. But I'm not sure about the staff. They do tend to shout a lot and criticise'; and [the school] 'is calm and disciplined, with a strict dress code. It is 'a shouting environment'. A new head had taken a stand against this, and in this governor's view, standards of discipline had deteriorated as a result, because the pupils are no longer frightened of the staff. In a two form entry primary school 'we've got a top and a bottom [group], and within those groups they're split as well ... God help the poor child who is at the bottom of the class'.

Only a minority of governing bodies seems to monitor this aspect of school life, which seems essential to the integrity of a Catholic school. There is a view that to do so is wrong: '[i]f you start creating committees like that, somehow or other, the people that monitor that bit are the parish priest or people who are seen as particularly local Catholic worthies ... I wouldn't encourage that because I would say it's a corporate responsibility'. On the other hand, if you do not have a specific mechanism for monitoring, and rely on the conviction that, if all is not well, the governing body will hear about it somehow, examples such as the ones I have given above will go unchallenged. At a recent meeting a primary head described to her governors the various steps she had taken to avoid accepting an unruly pupil who had been excluded from a neighbouring school. In this instance, one of the governors (who had been a LA officer, and therefore was perhaps more used to dealing with these things) responded 'And what would Jesus say?' But in how many schools would such a challenge take place?

My research also showed up other areas of concern. In the face of the ever-present shortage of Catholic teachers to fill key posts in Catholic schools, a significant number of governors were prepared to ignore the Bishops Conference policy on the matter. How enforceable this policy now is must be open to question since the bishops have long taken no action when Catholic independent schools breach it. As I write, I have before me an advertisement in *Tablet* that reads 'the preference is for the Head … to be a practising Catholic' rather than 'applicants should be practising Catholics'. As an experienced diocesan commissioner has said: 'if you're a faith community, where the fundamental core purpose is to pass on the faith', if you haven't got it, I really don't know how you can properly begin to understand the model…What right have you to lead a faith community?'.

My conclusion is that there needs to be a redoubling of effort by trustees to promote the Catholic perspective for governors, and that they should recognise more fully than they appear to at the moment the decisive role that governors can play in the evangelising work of the church. Specifically, they should encourage governors to get to know the wealth of material that is already available to help them. As many acknowledge, the Catholic school is the only regular experience of church that many children and young people (not to mention their parents) now have.

Notes

1   Education Act 1980 (UK). See: http://www.legislation.gov.uk/ukpga/1980/20/section/4/enacted.

2   Catholic Education Service for England and Wales Digests of Census Data: See: http://www.catholiceducation.org.uk/ces-census.

3   G. Grace, *Catholic Schools: Mission, Markets and Morality* (London: Routledge Falmer, 2002).

4   The Department for Education (DfE) and the Office for Standards in Education (Ofsted).

5   T. Piketty, *Capital in the Twenty-First Century* (Cambridge, Massachusetts, London: Belknap Harvard, 2014).

6   Congregation for Catholic Education, *The Catholic School* (1977); *Lay Catholics in Schools: Witnesses to Faith* (1982); *The Religious Dimension of Education in a Catholic School* (1988) and *The Catholic School on the Threshold of the Third Millennium* (1998).

7   Congregation for Catholic Education, *The Catholic School*, 34.

8   *Ibid.*, 37.

9   *Ibid.*, 39.

10 *Ibid.*, 45.

11 Congregation for Catholic Education, The *Catholic School on the Threshold* (1998), 10.

12 *Ibid.*, 14.

13 Catholic Bishops' Conference of England and Wales, *Spiritual and Moral Development Across the Curriculum* (London: Catholic Education Service, 1995); *The Common Good in Education* (London, Catholic Education Service, 1997); *Governing a Catholic School* (London: Catholic Education Service, 1998); Catholic Education Service, *Evaluating the Distinctive Nature of a Catholic School* (London: Catholic Education Service, 1999).

14 Catholic Bishops' Conference of England and Wales, *Spiritual and Moral Development*, 1995, 13–14.

15 Catholic Education Service, *The Common Good in Education* (London: CES, 1997), 6–14.

16 T. H. McLaughlin, *Parental Rights in Religious Upbringing and Religious Education within a Liberal Perspective* (London: University of London unpublished PhD Thesis, 1990).

17 C. Storr, *Serving Two Masters? Catholic School Governors at Work* (Leominster: Gracewing, 2011).

18 LA is the abbreviation for Local Authority.

13 INITIAL AND ON-GOING FORMATION OF CATHOLIC SCHOOL TEACHERS AND LEADERS—A PERSPECTIVE FROM THE UK

Dr John Lydon

Dr John Lydon is Director of the MA in Catholic School Leader-ship, St Mary's University, London and he is Professor and Co-Director of an undergraduate programme of the University of Notre Dame. He is currently involved in the establishment of a global Masters in Catholic school leadership with Australian Catholic University. He was appointed thematic expert of the Catholic-Inspired NGO Forum for education working in partner-ship with the Vatican Secretariat of State. He is a member of the Executive of the World Union of Catholic Teachers and the Catholic Association of Teachers Schools and Colleges (UK).

Abstract

After a brief introduction outlining the provenance of the Masters in Catholic School Leadership introduced at St Mary's University, Twickenham in 1997, this chapter discusses the nature of the programme, highlighting its demonstrable focus on formation, focusing especially on building community and the sacramental perspective before underlining contemporary challenges. The chapter concludes by documenting a new innovation created by the author which addresses the formation of aspiring early career leaders, recognised as such by their headteachers. This is proving popular in the new era of academisation when responsibility for formation is increasingly in the hands of the directors of the multi-academy trusts.

The Provenance of the Masters in Catholic School Leadership

In the preparatory document to the World Congress on Catholic Education which took place in 2015 in Rome, the importance of preparation for Catholic School Leadership was highlighted:

> ... a particular attention must be devoted *to the formation and selection of school heads.* They are not only in charge of their respective schools, but are also Bishops' reference persons inside schools in matters of pastoral care. School heads must be leaders who make sure that education is a shared and living mission, who support and organise teachers, who promote mutual encouragement and assistance.[1]

The MA in Catholic School Leadership: Principles and Practice was launched at St Mary's University, London in September 1997, 18 years before the Congress, as a part-time programme of advanced professional development aimed at experienced teachers who were either already in leadership roles in Catholic schools or who aspired to take on such work. It was the first such course in the UK. Indeed, in the English-speaking world at that time, one would have to travel to the USA or to Australia to find anything parallel being offered. There has been an exponential growth in numbers since the initial 22 students embarked upon the programme. There are currently over 150 students engaged through a variety of modes of study including a range of centres were students are involved in 'blended learning'. Students are also offered the opportunity to engage via a full distance learning mode as well as a full-time mode which involves, primarily, international students.

One of the principal aims of the programme constitutes the provision of a vocationally oriented programme of academic rigour that facilitates students in integrating a Catholic philosophy of education with the principles and practice of school leadership. This encompasses the formation of current and future leaders of Catholic schools alongside the formation of leaders who may, in the future, adopt a Catholic philosophy of education in leading community schools. The programme is open to Catholic teachers and leaders and colleagues of other faiths and beliefs. The programme is not, solely, concerned with preparation for headship but recognises that all teachers are leaders and therefore seeks to offer vocational and professional formation to all who aspire to leadership across phases. Theological literacy, regarded as a gap in provision by Dioceses across England and Wales, features prominently in the programme.

Formation for Leadership—Building Community

> Prime responsibility for creating the unique school climate rests with the teachers as individuals and as a community. The religious dimension of the school climate is expressed through the celebration of Christian values in Word and Sacrament, in individual behaviour, in friendly and harmonious personal relationships, and in a ready availability. Through this daily witness, the students will come to appreciate the uniqueness of the environment to which their youth has been entrusted.[2]

This iconic pronouncement, cited in school mission statements and leadership programmes internationally, reflects one of the key ecclesiological principles emanating from Vatican II in the context of the leadership of Catholic schools. The powerful assertion that prime responsibility rests with teachers as a community reflects the principle of collaborative ministry which features strongly both in conciliar and post-conciliar documents. The word 'community', for example, is cited 24 times in the document quoted above. The MA programme emphasises the centrality of community by retrieving a wide range of scholarship and Church pronouncements to exemplify the assertion that 'in their own individual ways all members of the school community share the Christian vision, makes the school 'Catholic'.[3] Gerald Grace, for example, quoting the seminal work of researchers who conducted a major study of Catholic schooling in the USA suggests:

> They [Bryk et al.,] argued that Catholic schools are
> informed by 'an inspirational ideology' (301) which makes
> them qualitatively different from public (state) schools.
> This inspirational ideology celebrates the primacy of the
> spiritual and moral life; the dignity of the person; the
> importance of community and moral commitments to
> caring, social justice and the common good.[4]

While an exploration of the wide-ranging nature of a school
community is beyond the scope of this article, it is worthy of note
that the axial nature of the home-school-parish partnership
features strongly, including an exploration of the contemporary
challenges in the current climate described as 'fragmented
Catholicity'.[5] In this context Bryk would argue that the way in
which teachers and leaders model community is critical:

> Collegiality among teachers represents another important
> structural component in a communal school organisation.
> Catholic school faculty spend time with one another both
> inside and outside of school. Social interactions serve as a
> resource for problem solving and contribute to *adult
> solidarity around the school mission*. In such contexts
> school decision-making is less conflictual and more often
> characterised by mutual trust and respect.[6]

There is supporting evidence from student evaluations that the
MA programme not only offers a programme of formation within
which the nature of 'community' features strongly but actually
models community. Apart from the collegial nature of student-
tutor interactions, the discussion forum facility within the Virtual
Learning Environment (VLE) is used to offer up to 15 learning
activities for each module. All students, whatever their mode of
study or wherever they are based, engage with these activities in
one online learning community per module. This means that the
'lone' Full Distance Learning student is able to join in discussions
about aspects of leadership theory and practice and to share their
critical analysis of literature sources and on current challenges
being faced within schools nationally and internationally. Feed-

back received from students indicates that, through a blended learning experience, they enjoy not only conventional aspects of academic study, but also online learning activities, which afford them the opportunity to share experiences asynchronously with others both in the UK and abroad. Thus, the learning experience of students on the programme is enhanced by their engagement with other students online in a virtual learning environment

Formation for Leadership—the Sacramental Perspective

The concept of modelling forms a perennial theme permeating all facets of the MA programme. Modelling ministry on Christ, the sacramental perspective, constitutes the foundation on which this programme is built, encapsulated in a further Congregation document:

> Conduct is always much more important than speech ...
> It is in this context that the faith witness of the lay teacher
> becomes especially important. Students should see in their
> teachers the Christian attitude and behaviour that is often
> so conspicuously absent from the secular atmosphere in
> which they live.[7]

This document explores the importance of nurturing the vocation and spirituality of the teacher. It articulates the significance for young people of role models who reflect in their lives what it means to be a disciple of Jesus. It is the second post-conciliar document to officially recognise 'the decline in religious personnel which has had such a profound effect on Catholic schools, especially in some countries'.[8] The document, therefore, emphasises the increasing importance of lay people in the ministry of teaching. The specific quotation above reflects the words of Pope Paul VI that teachers are listened to only when they are witnesses.[9] By emphasising the importance of witness this document is reflecting a sacramental perspective. Ways in which the individual teacher can give concrete witness to discipleship are explored in the programme, relating particularly to servant leadership, *the* classically Christian leadership model emphasising that, to be credible, teachers and leaders should demonstrate a commitment that is 'vigorous rather than virtual, substantial as opposed to superficial'.[10]

When discussing ways in which an individual can give concrete witness are discussed, engagement in extra-curricular activities often holds centre stage. St Paul's reference to Christ 'taking the form of a servant' (Ph 2:5–11) is particularly evocative in its resonance with the way in which such engagement reflects 'self-emptying' on the part of the teacher. The extent to which this engagement contributes to the enhancing of the student-teacher relationship and, de-facto, to the building of a strong school community, is incontrovertible, evidenced in research such as that by the author in his exploration of the concept of teaching as a vocation.ix[11] In that study several teachers suggested that the self-sacrificing nature of some teachers was their abiding institutional memory of their school days and the aspect of the teaching vocation most worthy of emulation. The value of extra-curricular engagement in building student confidence and a 'family atmosphere' in schools constitutes the distinctive contribution of St John Bosco (1815–88) to a philosophy of Catholic education.[12]

While appearing on the surface to be disarmingly simplistic, Pope Francis, at the recent World Congress, highlighted it as a particularly significant characteristic for Catholic schools of the 21st century. Citing the example of Bosco's integration of formal and extra-curricular activities into one educational synthesis in support of his assertion that education was in danger of being impoverished by an over-emphasis on academic outcomes the Holy Father suggested that:

> We need new horizons and new models. We need to open up horizons for an education that is not just in the head. There are three languages: head, heart, and hand. Education must pass through these three pathways. We must

help them to think, feel what is in their hearts, and help them in doing. So these three languages must be in harmony with each other.[13]

Contemporary Challenges

The increasing focus on what could be term performativity, alluded to by Pope Francis, has been discussed in other chapters. In the context of formation for leadership the advancing 'secular age' in the words of Charles Taylor[14], marked by a separating of religion from life, a falling off of religious practice and a postmodern culture that marginalises faith, is a, perhaps, greater challenge. If Grace Davie is right in suggesting that Europe is marked by a culture of 'believing without belonging'[15], characterised by a profound mismatch between religious values that people profess (believing), and actual churchgoing and religious practice (belonging), it could be at least postulated that the religious lives of a proportion of the overall number of Catholic teachers will not be practising Catholics in the way that term is understood traditionally. While it may be an overstatement to suggest that the majority have moved from an institutionally Catholic identity to a more autonomous search for spirituality, one of the key questions for Catholic school leaders revolves around the promotion and maintenance of Catholic identity as an empowering and motivating reality. In other words a critical moment has been reached when there is a need to move from defining this distinctive identity to researching effective means of sustaining it. While I am convinced that modelling ministry on Christ particularly by Catholic school leaders will always be the primary source of empowerment, formation such as that offered by the MA in Catholic school leadership programme, with its integration of theology, management studies and education, constitutes a significant support to the maintenance of Catholic identity in the current educational climate. The number of colleagues who have proceeded to lead schools across sectors and indeed internationally bears testimony to this assertion.

Shepherding Talent—a New Innovation

Notwithstanding the author's conviction that the MA in Catholic School Leadership programme continues to make a significant impact on the formation of Catholic school leaders, he is aware that not all aspiring leaders are at a point in their careers when they are equipped to embark upon study at Masters Level. With this in mind, and following consultations with key constituencies, he has developed *Shepherding Talent,* a programme in which teachers identified as having potential for leadership are challenged to explore their vocation to lead. Through workshops, the mission of the Catholic educator is elucidated alongside a consideration of personal disposition and values, inviting a critically reflective response to leadership. Based on the conviction that having a vocation and being a professional are, in essence, simply aspects of the pathway of discipleship, the programme encompasses professional, theological and spiritual paradigms. The programme has been structured to incorporate the potential of offering 30 credits towards an MA in Catholic leadership or a related discipline. Student evaluations have suggested that opportunities have been afforded to reflect on the importance and relevance of a Catholic school in a community and indeed to reflect on students' role within their school. They also spoke of an increased awareness of the attributes and behaviour for successful leadership while suggesting the course has served as a reminder of the call to serve modelled on Christ's ministry. Developments going forward will focus on more of the current pressures on schools from government and how a Catholic school can cope without losing its identity while liaising more closely with nominating schools to integrate professional progression with formation.

Conclusion

In the introductory chapter of this book, dignity and the call to human flourishing were signposted as two core principles in the context of contemporary Catholic education. The exploration of the sacramental perspectives within both the MA and *Shepherding Talent* programmes emphasises that one of the goals of every Catholic education institute should be to ensure that pupils experience their 'dignity as a person before he knows its definition'.[16] The nature of Jesus' ministry is broken open into constituent elements including invitation, inclusion, respect for an individual's discernment and presence and participants are challenged to reflect upon the extent to which they witness to these aspects. Aspiring leaders are also challenged to reflect upon the importance of school as a community modelled on that of the earliest Christian communities and to recognise the genuine human flourishing can be developed only in that context. The role of the virtual learning environment cannot be understated in this context. Student evaluations are replete with references to the value of building a virtual community of leaders and learners and the way in which this dialogue has impacted on their practice. One student spoke of:

> My practice has changed as I am now far more reflective in my dealings with both staff and students. I think about how my behaviour and professional demeanour might be understood not only in light of the context of education but also in the context of education within a Catholic school.[17]

The challenges faced in the current educational climate are discussed robustly. Students on both programmes are challenged to discern the symbiotic relationship between vocation and provision and to view the quest for academic standards as part of a spiritual quest, as one aspect of a search for excellence in Christians are called to seek perfection 'in all aspects of their lives.'[18] Participants are encouraged to discern that the seeking of perfection, analogous to human flourishing, applies to leaders, teachers and students and that by engaging in lifelong learning they are modelling for their own students a commitment that is canonised in the ministry of Jesus. Students are encouraged to reflect upon the fact that, in the current secular milieu, the most important commitment of any school leader is his or her witness to the Catholic faith tradition. Such a commitment will act as a powerful source of 'spiritual capital', defined by Grace as 'resources of faith and values derived from commitment to a religious tradition'.[19]

Grace is, in effect, expressing a certain quality which he had encountered when interviewing his sample of headteachers, a quality which becomes a 'source of empowerment because it provides a transcendent impulse which can guide judgement and action in the mundane world',[20] thus resonating with a third core principle of this book, the promise of a divine destiny. Students of both programmes have commented insistently on their value in keeping at the forefront the primary reason for the Catholic Church's engagement in its education mission encompassing more than 140,000 schools and Universities throughout the world. In the midst of the contemporary challenges alluded to earlier the primary reason was articulated by the Congregation for Catholic Education in its most recent publication, words that constitute a fitting conclusion to this chapter:

> At the heart of Catholic education there is always Jesus Christ: everything that happens in Catholic schools and universities should lead to an encounter with the living Christ. If we look at the great educational challenges that we will face soon, we must keep the memory of God made flesh in the history of mankind—in our history—alive.[21]

Notes

[1]   Congregation for Catholic Education, *Educating Today and Tomorrow: A Renewing Passion* (2014), III (emphasis added).

[2]   Congregation for Catholic Education, *The Religious Dimension of Education in a Catholic School* (1988), 26.

[3]   Congregation for Catholic Education, *The Catholic School* (1977), 34.

[4]   G. Grace, *School Leadership: Beyond Education Management* (London: Falmer Press, 1995), 159 quoting A. S. Bryk, P. B. Holland & V. E. Lee,

Catholic Schools and the Common Good (Cambridge MA: Harvard University Press, 1993), 301.

5   A. Casson, *Fragmented Catholicity and Social Cohesion: Faith Schools in a Plural Society* (Oxford, Peter Lang Publishing, 2012).

6   Bryk *et al.*, *Catholic Schools*, 299 (emphasis added).

7   Congregation for Catholic Education, *Lay Catholics in Schools: Witnesses to Faith* (1982), 32.

8   *Ibid.*, 3.

9   Pope Paul VI., Pope Apostolic Exhortation *Evangelii Nuntianti* (1975), 41.

10 J. Sullivan, 'Leadership and Management'. In: M. A. Hayes & L. Gearon (eds), *Contemporary Catholic Schools in the United Kingdom* (Leominster: Gracewing, 2002), 93.

11 See J. Lydon, *The Contemporary Catholic Teacher: A Reappraisal of the Concept of Teaching as a Vocation in the Catholic Christian Context* (Saarbrucken, Germany: Lambert Academic Publishing, 2011).

12 *Ibid.*, 251.

13 Congregation for Catholic Education, World Congress Final Communique (21 November 2015)

14 C. Taylor, *A Secular Age* (Cambridge MA: Harvard University Press, 2007).

15 G. Davie, *Religion in Britain since 1945: Believing without Belonging* (Oxford: Blackwell, 1994).

16 Congregation for Catholic Education, *The Catholic School* (1977).

17 Student Module Evaluation (Twickenham: St Mary's University, 2015).

18 Catholic Bishops Conference of England & Wales, *Principles, Practices and Concerns* (London: CES, 1996).

19 G. Grace, *Catholic Schools: Mission, Markets and Morality* (London: Falmer Press, 2002), 236.

20 *Ibid.*, 236.

21 Congregation for Catholic Education, *Educating Today and Tomorrow* (2014), III.

Lightning Source UK Ltd.
Milton Keynes UK
UKHW011006070421
381574UK00001B/256

9 780852 449332